THE STRESS
MANAGEMENT KIT

THE STRESS

MANAGEMENT KIT

ALIX NEEDHAM

CONNECTIONS
BOOK PUBLISHING

To my ongoing love affair with India, my spiritual home.

A CONNECTIONS EDITION
First published in Great Britain in 1996 by Virgin Books
The previous edition comprised book, stress sensor dots and audiotape

This edition published in Great Britain in 2002 by
Connections Book Publishing Limited
St Chad's House, 148 King's Cross Road, London WC1X 9DH

British Library Cataloguing-in-Publication data available on request.

ISBN 1-85906-070-6

1 3 5 7 9 10 8 6 4 2

Phototypeset in Stymie using QuarkXPress on Apple Macintosh
Printed and bound in Hong Kong by Magnum Offset Printing Co. Limited

Contents

Introduction

We all know what it feels like to be so exhausted we cannot sleep, our heads spinning with things we should have done, or to feel overwhelmed and unable to cope with work and family. Stress can get to all of us and the reason you have picked up this book is because you want to do something positive about it.

Stress can be caused by many different factors – work, bereavement, traffic jams, and noise, for example – and it can affect people in numerous ways. With *The Stress Management Kit*, you will learn how to control the different elements that cause you stress and you will also discover how to reduce the actual stress you feel to an acceptable level.

How to use The Stress Management Kit

The Stress Management Kit offers you a dynamic, three-pronged approach to effective stress management. It comprises a book, two Stressdots®, and a relaxation CD. Here is a guide to using the three elements so that you can get maximum benefit from them all.

The book

The bulk of the book is divided into two parts. The chapters in Part One will help you identify and understand the sources of stress in your life. In the course of reading through, you may be surprised to learn that the goal of the kit is not to eliminate all stress from your life – some stress is actually good for you and life without any stress at all would be impossibly dull!

Because we are all different, it is important to find the level and types of stress that bother you. To help you do this, Part One contains numerous quizzes and questionnaires that are designed to help you assess your life honestly. After you have pinpointed the areas that need to be worked on to get rid of the negative effects of stress, you can move on to Part Two which shows you how to take positive action.

In Part Two, you will learn how to manage, control and overcome the negative effects of stress. There is no single approach to dealing with stress, so in this section you will find methods and suggestions for reducing and controlling the strains of everyday life – you can choose those which are most appropriate for you. Some of the exercises ask you to write things down. You may think that this is crass or unnecessary but it is not. By jotting things down, you show yourself commitment and provide yourself with written statements which are easier to act on than nebulous thoughts. Writing things down is crucial to combatting stress successfully.

Part Two will also help you to develop a lifestyle that will improve your resistance to – and safeguard you from – stress-induced illness. Chapter Sixteen at the end of the book is a quick-reference summary of Parts One and Two.

At the back of the book, after Part Two, there is Gaining Further Help, a section where you will find invaluable information on where to go and who to see if you feel you want professional help. As well as contact addresses, it contains lists of useful recordings and books.

The Stressdots®

These dots are small adhesive discs that you stick to your wrist where they change colour in response to your stress levels. They are invaluable aids and will help you identify and monitor the stress in your life. In Chapter Two, you will learn how these unique devices can be incorporated into your stress management programme. If you need more dots, order them from the addresses given in Gaining Further Help.

The CD

The purpose of the CD is to help you to relax. You can listen to it during your lunch break or in the evening when you get home from work – in fact at virtually any time when you feel tense and wound up (not, however, when you are driving or operating machinery). Full instructions on the use of the CD are given in Chapter Twelve.

Once you are familiar with its contents, you can treat *The Stress Management Kit* rather like a tool box – you can dip into it and use the sections you need, exactly when you need them.

Chapter One

Identifying the Causes of Stress

The aim of this chapter is to illustrate just how many causes of stress there are and to show you that many of them may be affecting you without you even realizing it. For example, you may think that the only stress you really consider relevant in your life is pressure at work or perhaps the aggravation of having to pick up your children every day at a time when you would rather be relaxing. But there is usually more to it than that and any bad experiences you may be feeling as a result of stress will probably be for a mixture of reasons. Read through the chapter and make notes in the various questionnaires. This will help you to isolate and identify the roots of the stresses and strains you feel. Armed with this self-knowledge, you will be in a better position to tackle any problems you may have.

Unfortunately, there is no simple definition of stress. When we talk about stress, we could be talking about a combination of the circumstances or conditions – the 'stressors' – that cause it, or we could be talking about the effects of the stressors.

Stressors come in any number of forms but they are usually life events or situations that spin out of your control. Getting stuck in a traffic jam on the way to a job interview is an example of a stressor; collecting a parking ticket because you were in too much of a hurry to read the restrictions is another.

Stress is what you feel in response to stressors. You may feel a sense of panic as you sit helplessly behind the wheel as you inch your way towards your interview appointment; or you may feel angry and frustrated that you are obliged to pay a large parking fine.

There is another way of putting it: stress can be thought of as the perception that events or circumstances have challenged or exceeded your ability to cope. It is important to point out at this stage, however, that there are two common misconceptions about stress. One is that it is an external factor – something

8

that *happens* to you, like blaming your boss for your problems at work. The other is that stress is always a *bad* thing. In the first case, quite the reverse is true. Stress is something that *you* create inside yourself – it is how you react to what is going on around you. And, in the second case, you may not want to believe it but some stress is actually healthy and good for you. So let us take a look at good and bad stress.

Positive, beneficial stress is what you feel after a day of gardening, a long day's shopping, or a busy week at work. All these are stimulating and rewarding. After a hot bath and a restful evening you feel recovered and happy with what you have achieved. If you view each task you do as a challenge then you will tend to generate stimulating stress, the kind of stress that spurs you on to achieve goals and get a job done.

Challenge or threat?

Regard the same tasks as a threat and you will trigger negative stress. Anger, frustration, anxiety and self-doubt are all examples of the emotions you feel when you experience negative stress. You may begin to think you cannot do a job, or that it is too much for you. If you experience negative stress for too long, it becomes something that leaves you feeling helpless and out of control. For better or worse, when we refer to stress in every day conversation, we nearly always are actually referring to negative stress.

Have you ever wondered why some people deal with stress better than others? Why it is that a colleague who is under the same pressure as you comes into work positively glowing, while you feel like a limp rag? It is invariably because your perception of an event, and your inability to cope with it, creates a negative stress response in you, whereas the same event triggers a positive response in your colleague. What you see as a problem is not viewed in the same way by your friend. In other words, it is not the event that determines whether or not you feel good or bad stress, it is how you respond to it.

Here is an example of how two people might respond differently to the same stressor.

Pat relishes a challenge and wants to organize a surprise silver wedding anniversary party for his parents. His sister, Julie, on the other hand, hates the idea and just thinking about it makes her hands go clammy.

Arranging the party is something Pat would choose to do whereas Julie would only do it if she was forced into it. This element of choice is another key factor in whether or not a task becomes negatively stressful.

How much control you think you have over an event or situation and the question of choice play the most crucial roles in determining your response to a stressor. If deadlines at work mean you *have* to work late when you would rather be out living it up with friends, or if you feel *obliged* to take your mother to the airport, then you will respond and feel very differently than if you *chose* to work late so that you could take a long weekend, or if you *offered* to take your mother to the airport in order to catch up with family news.

Causes of stress   Thinking of stressors in different categories will help you to become aware of the variety that there are in your life. This is an important step – it is only when you have identified the stressors that apply to you, that you can realistically hope to control their effects.

As you read through the different categories listed below, think about how each stressor may be affecting your life. Which ones apply to you? When you complete the charts, it is crucially important to be as honest with yourself as possible. This is not always as easy as it sounds, but it is only by being truthful with yourself that you will gain genuine insight into the ways you think and feel.

Lifestyle stressors   These crop up in everyday life. Some may be beyond your control while others might appear to be insignificant but should not be ignored – they could easily build up over time and become a major source of negative stress.

Lifestyle stressors

Stressor	Yes	No
Getting stuck in traffic	X	
Exhaust fumes/air pollution		X
Interruptions at work	X	
The weather	X	
Noise at work or at home	X	
Waiting in queues	X	
Overcrowding	X	
Poor relationships	X	
Time pressure – too much/too little	X	
Financial difficulties	X	

Do any of the lifestyle stressors in the chart have a negative effect on you? Tick Yes or No.

Mind stressors

These influence the ways in which you think. How do you remember your past? If you only remember the bad bits then you will think that you had an unhappy childhood. How do you view your present and future experiences? If you can only remember the row you had with your neighbours, or a nasty letter from the bank manager, you will tend to label your life as unhappy and stressful.

Talking to yourself in a negative way, jumping to the wrong conclusions, taking things personally, exaggerating your problems – these are all mind stressors that can have a massive impact on the ways in which you behave and react to both people and situations. Dwelling on things that you *should*, *ought*, *must*, and *have to do*, can make you feel depressed, guilty, oversensitive and pressured. In short, mind stressors can make you feel so miserable and anguished that life becomes a struggle.

11

Do you feel that any of these statements (mind stressors) apply to you? Tick Yes or No.

Mind stressors

Stressor	Yes	No
I always have to be pleasant no matter how I feel	X	
I have to be the best at whatever I do		X
Unless I worry about things, they seem to get worse	X	
I ought to be able to cope on my own	X	
I must do everything perfectly		X
I cannot do much about my life		X
I often feel I am not good enough		X
I am the only one who can solve my problems		X
I will never be a success		X
Everyone is better than me		X

Body stressors Your physical condition also affects how well you deal with stress. Check the chart to discover what might be weakening your body and leaving you vulnerable to negative stress.

Tick Yes or No, depending on whether or not these body stressors apply to you.

Body stressors

Stressor	Yes	No
You are unfit	X	
You have had a recent accident		X
You have an unbalanced diet	X	

Body stressors (cont.)

Stressor	Yes	No
You have suffered a recent illness		X
You sleep badly	X	
You sometimes overeat or overdrink	X	
You smoke		X
You take drugs (e.g. sleeping tablets)		X
You neglect your body	X	

Overwork and poor staff management are now recognized as stressors. In the USA there has been a rise in employee compensation lawsuits due to occupational stress, and during the last few years British courts have awarded damages to employees who successfully claimed that their health had suffered due to work-related stress. Not surprisingly, many countries now have official guidelines aimed at reducing stress in the work place.

Work stressors

Work stressors

Stressor	Yes	No
You are overworked		X
You feel undervalued		X
There is too much office politics at your place of work		X
The demands of work are affecting your private life		X
Your work is under constant time pressure	X	

Do any of the work stressors listed left and overleaf apply to you? Tick Yes or No.

Work stressors (cont.)

Stressor	Yes	No
You are unhappy with what you are paid	X	
You do not have enough work to occupy your time		X
You have to manage people		X
You frequently take work home		X
You occasionally get into conflict with colleagues		X

Change stressors

Changes taking place in your life can be immensely stressful and can even lead to illness. If several changes occur at the same time, the effects can be compounded. For example, if you move house, start a new job, and have your partner's parents to stay for a month, all within a fairly short time span, the resulting stress burden will probably be huge.

In my work counselling people, I have observed that constant change, and the stress that it generates, can be related to the onset of illness any time within the following two-year period. It is usual to find that the more life events a person goes through, the worse their stress condition gets. Consequently, they find it harder than ever to get back to 'normal'.

This does not mean that you must never move, swap your job, or refuse to let the children leave home for fear of the ensuing stress it will create. No changes at all in your life lead to boredom which can be almost as bad as too much stress – too little change will leave you feeling stagnant and unfulfilled.

Just how important change stressors can be has been proved by two US researchers, Thomas Holmes, a psychiatrist, and Richard Rahe, a psychologist. During the course of their work, which was to explore the likelihood of illness developing in individuals as a direct result of stress, they found that the event consistently reported as being the most stressful was the death of a spouse. From this they compiled what they called a 'Life Stress Inventory'. They assigned bereavement a value of 100 and then established a sliding scale for over 40 more life events.

Read through the Holmes and Rahe values shown in the chart on page 16. Then, using their values as a guide, put your own score against the events you have experienced in the past year. If, for example, your son going to away to university was a happy occasion, you might decide to give the event less than the 29 points that Holmes and Rahe have awarded it. If it was a very traumatic occasion, you can give it a higher score.

After filling in the chart, add up your scores. This total will give you an idea of the amount of stress you have experienced in the last year. The higher your score, the greater the likelihood is of you becoming ill in the next year.

If you scored more than 151 units, you should see your doctor for regular medical checkups. In this way you will be able to monitor any signs of illness that may be developing and will be able to receive appropriate treatment. It must be remembered, though, that lifestyle changes alone are not enough to cause illness. As you have already learnt, it is your perception of these changes that makes the difference.

The goal of stress management

The Holmes and Rahe Inventory deals mainly with major events, but seemingly minor stressors that occur day in, day out, can be just as stressful. Dr Richard Lazarus, a researcher at the University of California at Berkeley, has determined that everyday hassles, like getting stuck in a traffic jam, waiting for a bus, losing your house keys, and disagreements at work, have a greater impact on your wellbeing than you might think.

It is when hassles build up over time that they become a problem. Unlike change stressors that are often isolated from one another with a gap between during which you can adjust to the change, hassles constantly nag and irritate.

The values listed in the chart are Holmes and Rahe indicators. Opposite events that you have experienced in the last year, enter your own scores. These may be more or less than the indicators.

Just how stressful these hassles become depends on a variety of factors – your coping style, your personality, what the rest of the day was like, and the nature of the hassle itself. The ultimate aim of this book is to show you how you can manage the hassles and the changes, along with all the other stressors in your life. First, however, you have to know when you are suffering from stress. This is not as silly as it might sound, as you will discover when you read through the contents of Chapter Two.

Holmes and Rahe Inventory

Life Event	Value	Your score
Death of a spouse	100	
Divorce	73	
Marital separation	65	
Jail term	64	
Death of a close family member	63	
Personal injury or illness	53	
Marriage	50	
Fired at work	47	
Retirement	45	
Marital reconciliation	45	
Change in health of a family member	44	
Pregnancy	40	
Sex difficulties	39	
Gain of a new family member	39	
Change in financial state	38	
Death of a close friend	37	
Change to a different line of work	36	
Change in number of arguments with spouse	35	

Holmes and Rahe Inventory (cont.)

Life Event	Value	Your score
Mortgage over one year's net salary	31	
Foreclosure of mortgage or loan	30	
Change in responsibilities at work	29	
Son or daughter leaving home	29	
Trouble with in-laws	29	
Outstanding personal achievement	28	
Spouse begins or stops work	26	
Begin or end school	26	
Change in living conditions	25	
Revision in personal habits	24	
Trouble with boss	23	
Change in work hours or conditions	20	
Change in residence	20	
Change in schools	20	
Change in recreation	19	
Change in church activities	19	
Change in social activities	18	
Mortgage or loan less than one year's net salary	17	
Change in sleeping habits	16	
Change in number of family get-togethers	15	
Change in eating habits	15	
Vacation	13	
Christmas	13	
Minor violation of the law	11	
Miscellaneous		
Total score		

Chapter Two

Symptoms of Stress

So how can you tell whether you are really stressed or not? What are the signs? Everyone is different but there are certain patterns that crop up time and time again in people who are stressed. Among the most common statements my clients make are:'The smallest thing sets me off;' 'Life is all work and no play these days;' and 'I feel tense nearly all of the time.'

Recognize some of these feelings? If any of them apply to you then stress could be controlling your life.

Recognizing your symptoms The symptoms of stress manifest themselves in many ways. Some may even surprise you because you may just accept them as part of everyday life or you may be so accustomed to them that you ignore them altogether. Learning how to notice your stress symptoms is part of the key to successful stress management. In just the same way that you know when you are getting a cold and take some aspirin or get an early night to 'nip it in the bud', being aware of your particular set of stress symptoms will help you know when negative stress is setting in. If you spot the symptoms early enough, you can do something about the stress.

Evolution has designed us to defend ourselves instinctively from physical threats to our safety. When confronted by a grizzly bear, a caveman had to react quickly and the so-called 'fight or flight' response developed. The fight or flight response is a series of instantaneous physiological reactions that include: an increase in the flow of adrenaline, an increase in muscle tension, and an increase in heart rate.

'Present-day stressors trigger the same physiological changes in our bodies as marauding grizzlies did in our ancestors. But, because most stressors do not present us with a physical threat, we do not act as our bodies are designed. Instead of releasing all that pent-up energy in action by running out of the office

18

or supermarket screaming for help, we plough on regardless, causing emotions like frustration, anger and bitterness to fester. When this happens consistently over a period of days, weeks, months or even years, the negative stress reactions become unhealthy.

How stressed are you?

You may already know that you are stressed but do you know to what degree? The following exercises are designed to help you find out how stressed you are.

Each questionnaire focuses on a particular type of stress: physical, psychological and behavioural. Once you have completed all three you will have a much clearer picture of what area of your life stress hits hardest.

How does stress affect you physically?

This exercise will help you to find out what your physical stress symptoms are. Think about how often you experience the feelings listed in the chart and circle the number that most accurately represents how often these physical symptoms occur.

How does stress affect you physically?

	A	B	C	D	E
Headache	1	2	3	4	5
Heart Pounding	1	2	3	4	5
Allergy	1	2	3	4	5
Indigestion	1	2	3	4	5
Grinding teeth	1	2	3	4	5
Neckache	1	2	3	4	5
Backache	1	2	3	4	5
Fatigue/exhaustion	1	2	3	4	5
Sweaty hands and feet	1	2	3	4	5
Stomachache	1	2	3	4	5
Trembling	1	2	3	4	5
Tightness in chest	1	2	3	4	5
Score					

Against each of these physical symptoms, ring just one number. Pick a number that best represents how often the symptom occurs. Tally up your total number of points at the end.

KEY TO CHART

A= Never

B= Infrequently (more than once in six months)

C= Occasionally (more than once per month)

D= Very often (more than once per week)

E= Constantly

Fight or flight response

LEVEL OF STRESS

Pulse

Blood pressure

Blood sugar

Blood fats

Respiration

Sweating

Pupil dilation

The fight or flight response prepares the body for immediate action.

How does stress affect you psychologically?

This exercise will help you to find out how you think and feel when stressed. Circle the number that best represents your situation.

Circle the number that best represents how often these psychological symptoms occur and then add up your score.

How does stress affect you psychologically?

	A	B	C	D	E
Difficulty relaxing	1	2	3	4	5
Easily angered	1	2	3	4	5
Bored	1	2	3	4	5
Difficulty in concentrating	1	2	3	4	5
Difficulty with decisions	1	2	3	4	5
Anxious thoughts	1	2	3	4	5
Frustration	1	2	3	4	5
Hostility	1	2	3	4	5
Impatience	1	2	3	4	5
Racing thoughts	1	2	3	4	5
Sleeping difficulties	1	2	3	4	5
Loss of emotional control	1	2	3	4	5
Score					

KEY TO CHART

A = Never

B = Infrequently (more than once in six months)

C = Occasionally (more than once per month)

D = Very often (more than once per week)

E = Constantly

This exercise will help you to find out how you behave in stressful situations. Think for a few moments about your behaviour recently with your family, colleagues and friends before circling the responses that best fit your situation.

How does stress affect your behaviour?

Circle the number that best represents how often these behavioural traits apply to you. Add up your score on completion.

	A	B	C	D	E
Treat yourself to something new	1	2	3	4	5
Throw yourself into your work	1	2	3	4	5
Go quiet	1	2	3	4	5
Avoid being with people	1	2	3	4	5
Sexual difficulties	1	2	3	4	5
Find it difficult to laugh	1	2	3	4	5
Eat more or less than usual	1	2	3	4	5
Smoke/drink more than usual	1	2	3	4	5
Drive recklessly	1	2	3	4	5
Try to avoid situations	1	2	3	4	5
Use medications for physical symptoms	1	2	3	4	5
Take time off work	1	2	3	4	5
Score					

KEY TO CHART

A= Never

B= Infrequently (more than once in six months)

C= Occasionally (more than once per month)

D= Very often (more than once per week)

E= Constantly

Understanding your scores

Once you have completed all three questionnaires, add the three totals together to get a combined score. This figure is the key to understanding your stress load. You may have scored evenly across all three sections but the likelihood is that you scored much higher in one. It is crucially important to be aware of this – if you know where your stress is coming from, it is a great deal easier to do something positive about it. The higher your tally, the more likely you are to be suffering from overload.

Over 150

If you scored over 150 and this is fairly representative of your situation over a period of years, or even just months, then your stress problem is quite severe. You are fast approaching 'burnout'. If you do not do something to improve your damaging lifestyle immediately, you could be on the way to a nervous breakdown or paving the way for illness. You would benefit from seeing your doctor or seeking help from a professional counsellor. You definitely need to follow some of the stress management exercises in Part Two.

Between 110 and 149

Your stress levels are too high. You may be going through a crisis or major change in life. If so, do not worry too much as your body is designed for handling short-term stress and your score may simply represent such a period in your life. Try to focus on the issues that are causing you problems and try to deal with them one at a time or seek professional help from a counsellor. Choose the exercises in Part Two that are most appropriate to your situation – if you do not take positive action now, you could be putting your health at serious risk.

Between 90 and 109

Your stress levels are moderate. You are not in the danger zone yet but you could be if you do not take care. If you scored five in any area, you could be experiencing stress carried over from past events. Unresolved issues and unfinished business, which may have happened years before, can cause just as much stress as present issues. If this sounds familiar, try to identify and address the problems. If you are unhappy about tackling them on your own, then you may benefit from seeing a counsellor.

Below 90

You show few signs of stress. This low score could mean that you have struck the right balance as you seem to be coping well with whatever stressors you encounter. But you must remember that this is only a reading for your present stress level so do not rest on your laurels. You picked up this kit for a good reason, so be aware that something could happen next week which could send your score sky high.

Your low score could also be a sign of being under-stressed; this can be as much of a problem as too much stress. Symptoms of this can include lethargy and boredom. If you feel this represents your situation, you may find it beneficial to add a little zip to your life by seeking out more stimulating experiences. But do read on – learning how to relax and understanding other stress management techniques will help you to build up your energy reserves for when you need them.

Now that you have a general idea of what causes stress and how you deal with it, the next step is to tune in and really look at how you react to stressors from day to day. The best and most revealing way of doing this is to keep a 'stress diary'.

Making a stress diary

Keeping a record of the events that create stress, as well as your reactions to them, will help you to pinpoint the biggest stressors in your life. In Part Two of the book you will learn how to apply appropriate stress management techniques to deal with particular events.

In your diary, make a note of the time a stressful event occurs and also jot down how you felt. Your diary should look something like this:

Date: Friday, June 4

Time	Stressful event	How I felt
7.30am	Alarm didn't go off	Irritated
8.00am	Rushing for the bus	Headache
10.30am	Disagreement with Jim	Angry/stomach tension
11.00am	No milk left for tea	Furious
12.30pm	lunch date cancelled	Disappointed

Keep your diary for a week. It will help you to spot any patterns and you will see how particular stressors produce predictable symptoms. For example, rushing may make you feel irritable or give you a headache, and interpersonal difficulties may result in that all-to-familiar knotted stomach. Stick to keeping the diary if you possibly can – it may seem to be an additional hassle to start with but the results will prove invaluable.

How to use the Stressdots®

So far you have worked on identifying your present stress levels and recognizing your stress symptoms. But even armed with that information, it is easy to miss the signs of stress building up within you until you are having a row about whose turn it is to wash the dishes!

Stressdots® can play an invaluable role in stress management because they help you to recognize when your tension levels are increasing. They also give you the motivation to take positive action.

What are Stressdots®?

The Stressdots® are small self-adhesive discs which you place on the inside of your wrists. They change colour when you become tense and consequently give you immediate feedback on your stress levels. The dots are effective in most situations and you can wear them throughout the day for continuous monitoring at home, at work, while travelling or at meetings. There are, however, one or two provisos. For example, the dots may start changing colour if the ambient temperature is either very hot or very cold, or if you have just taken some exercise. Also, if you drink alcohol, your skin temperature will go up so the card may be fooled into giving false readings.

How do the Stressdots® work?

As we mentioned earlier, in any stressful situation your body goes into the fight or flight response that is designed to help you cope with a crisis. As part of this response, your blood supply is diverted away from the extremities and skin to the larger muscle groups – for example, the legs – where it is needed for action. With a reduced blood supply, the skin temperature of the hands and feet falls. The sensor works by monitoring

24

changes in your skin temperature, which fluctuates according to the amount of blood flowing through the skin. So, when you are tense and stressed, the blood vessels constrict, the blood flow to the skin is reduced, and the dots appear red, brown or black. When you are calm and relaxed, the blood vessels dilate, the blood flow to the skin is increased, and the dots appear green or blue.

How the Stressdots® work

Tense	Relaxed
Less blood flow to skin	More blood flow to skin
Skin cooler	Skin warmer
Dots turn red, brown or black	Dots turn green, blue or violet

By wearing the sensors you have a personal early warning system and a constant visual indicator of your tension levels – they provide a continuous flow of information throughout the day. Moreover, using the dots ensures that you cannot fool yourself into thinking that you are relaxed when you are not. This may sound ridiculous and you may think that feelings of stress are always obvious. Frequently, however, physical symptoms like headaches and stomach cramps are not recognized as symptoms of stress and are disregarded.

As the Stressdots® alert you at the earliest possible moment that tension is building up within you, you can take prompt action. By using the relaxation techniques suggested in Part Two, you can learn to calm yourself down as soon as you see the dots changing colour.

In short, the Stressdots® make it easier for you to control your stress levels. Ignore the warnings and pressure can build up, leading to symptoms described earlier or more serious disorders such as a weakened immune system. In Chapter Four we will look at the full impact of stress on health.

Chapter Three

The Link Between Stress and Personality

Everyone has their share of life's strains, pressures and misfortunes. But why is it that some people are more vulnerable than others to the stressors that life throws up at them? Some people seem to be permanently on edge and twitchy whereas others take everything in their stride and nothing appears to trouble them, even if they have high-pressure jobs with important responsibilites and problems at home as well.

By now, you will not be surprised to learn that one of the key factors that influences how vulnerable you are to stress is you – or more precisely your personality. Whether we like it or not, some personalities are more prone to suffering from stress than others – this trait is sometimes easier to see in friends and colleagues than in ourselves.

Two American researchers on a coronary prevention project, Drs Friedman and Rosenman, have identified two personality types which they have labelled 'Type A' and 'Type B'. Their research has shown that Type A personalities suffer significantly more coronary heart disease than Type B personalities.

The Type A personality has what Friedman and Rosenman called 'hurry sickness'. A typical Type A personality:

- always seems busy and runs his or her life by the clock;
- speaks quickly and loudly;
- walks quickly;
- eats rapidly;
- is impatient and irritable;
- tries do more than one thing at a time;
- feels guilty when relaxing;
- is competitive and plays to win;
- schedules too many activities into a day;
- and is intolerant of failure.

26

Not surprisingly, Type B individuals are the complete opposite. A typical Type B:

- can stay patient and calm;
- has no inner anger nor hostility;
- cooperates with others;
- can relax without feeling guilty;
- plays for fun, not to win;
- is flexible and easy going;
- and works without agitation.

In general, Type A men have higher blood fat levels than Type B and are six times more likely to have a heart attack. Similar health traits are found in Type A women. Type A business or professional women are around seven times more likely to suffer from coronary heart problems than Type B women who do not work.

How to assess your own Type A/Type B behaviour

The exercise overleaf will help you to ascertain whether you are a Type A or Type B personality. Read each statement and then answer it as honestly as possible by circling one number that best reflects the way you behave in your everyday life. For example, if you are generally on time for appointments, circle a number between 7 and 11; if you are usually casual about appointments, circle one of the lower numbers.

When you have finished, add up all the numbers you have circled to find your total score. Your total will be somewhere between 14 and 154. The highest score is 154 and signifies an extreme Type A, coronary-prone personality. A score of 14 signifies an extreme Type B personality.

It is important to remember that there are no absolute divisions between Type A and Type B but most people lean towards one type more than the other. The average score is 84 – a total above this means that you will tend to exhibit Type A traits, a total below is indicative of a Type B personality.

If you scored above 84 then it is important for you to learn how to manage your Type A behaviour. In Part Two you will find strategies to help you control your stress and so lessen your risk of illness. Circle one number for each statement which best reflects the way in which you behave in everyday life.

How to assess your own Type A/Type B behaviour

Type A		Type B
Never late	11 10 9 8 7 6 5 4 3 2 1	Bad timekeeping
Very competitive	11 10 9 8 7 6 5 4 3 2 1	Not competitive
Anticipates what others are going to say and interrupts	11 10 9 8 7 6 5 4 3 2 1	Good listener
Always feels under pressure	11 10 9 8 7 6 5 4 3 2 1	Never feels under pressure
Impatient while waiting	11 10 9 8 7 6 5 4 3 2 1	Waits patiently
Tries to do many things at once; thinks about what will do next	11 10 9 8 7 6 5 4 3 2 1	Takes one thing at a time
Loud in speech; fast and forceful	11 10 9 8 7 6 5 4 3 2 1	Takes time talking
Wants good job recognized by others	11 10 9 8 7 6 5 4 3 2 1	Cares about satisfying self no matter what others might think
Fast at doing things	11 10 9 8 7 6 5 4 3 2 1	Slow doing things
Hard driving (pushing self and others)	11 10 9 8 7 6 5 4 3 2 1	Easy-going
Hides feelings	11 10 9 8 7 6 5 4 3 2 1	Expresses feelings
Few interests outside work/home	11 10 9 8 7 6 5 4 3 2 1	Lots of hobbies/interests
Ambitious	11 10 9 8 7 6 5 4 3 2 1	Unambitious
Eager to get things done	11 10 9 8 7 6 5 4 3 2 1	Casual
Score		

We can all recognize the workaholic in the office. He or she is the one who arrives first in the morning and leaves last at night; the person who never has a lunch break and rarely takes a holiday; the one who will work at weekends and is prepared to cancel a night out without thinking twice. In short, the workaholic is obsessed with work.

The workaholic

Does any of this sound familiar? Could you be a workaholic? Although you may not have recognized the fact, your friends and family may already be convinced.

If you are a workaholic, the chances are that you did not start out as such. In fact, in the past, you may have been the first to suggest going out for a quick drink after work. But becoming obsessed with your work can creep up on you. It could be that your boss puts in more hours than anyone else so working over-time is expected and is no longer a one-off occurrence. And if you, like so many, have the possibility of redundancy looming over you, it is easy to start equating job security with the number of hours you put in.

The unsavoury truth is that you may not realize that you are a workaholic until it begins to make you ill. Workaholics notoriously avoid admitting that they are suffering from stress – being 'worked' makes them feel important and gives them a 'high'. When tensions and frustrations mount, workaholics merely redouble their efforts – they work even faster and put in even more hours. They push and push themselves until the unimaginable happens – their bodies finally give way and they have a breakdown or heart attack. Being able to cope with stress over a long period of time, workaholics begin to imagine that they are invincible. It is not uncommon for people who reach a stage of collapse to express surprise and say, 'I've always coped well before.' That, in a nutshell, is just the problem.

If you are a workaholic, you are not the only person who could end up suffering. Your family can pay a price for your behaviour too as it is they who have to take on extra responsibilities and carry out jobs that you should have done but avoided because you were at work. As a result, resentments and bitterness can boil over causing ructions and profound unhappiness.

To function effectively as a person, everyone needs time off work to relax and recharge their batteries. Working extended hours in an emergency, for a short time, can be stimulating. But driving yourself at full pace for months or years, without really being aware of what you are doing to yourself and to others, is potentially dangerous.

Are you a workaholic? Complete the questionnaire below as honestly as possible. From it, you will be able to determine whether or not work is taking over your life.

If you answer Yes to eight or more questions, you may be a workaholic and you need to make immediate changes to balance the amount of work and play in your life. Turn to Part Two where you will find exercises to help you counteract this obsessive behaviour.

Does work dominate your life? Tick Yes or No to the questions – if you record eight or more, you may be a workaholic.

Are you a workaholic?

Stressor	Yes	No
Do you get up early, no matter how late you go to bed?		
Do you work or read when you eat alone?		
Do you make daily lists of things to do?		
Do you find it difficult to 'do nothing'?		
Are you energetic and competitive		
Do you work on holidays and weekends?		
Can you work any time, anywhere?		
Do you find it difficult to take holidays?		
Do you dread retirement?		
Do you really enjoy your work?		

The hardy personality

It is a fact of life that some people are better at handling stress than others; some even seem to thrive on it! What is it that they have that perhaps you do not?

Actually, we need not one but three psychological qualities to help us become resilient to stress. These are termed the 'Three Cs': commitment, control, and a desire for challenge. People who possess all three of these qualities are sometimes referred to as 'hardy' personalities.

Do any of these sound like you?

- Commitment: You can accept challenges, yet still remain committed to both your job and your family life. You are active and keenly interested in life's opportunities. You identify the priorities in your life and commit yourself to those goals.
- Control: You believe that you can influence your work and home environments. You take charge of your life and make positive choices to deal with stressful events.
- Challenge: You see change as an opportunity or challenge – for you change is the spice of life. You believe that life always presents problems and that, once they have been challenged and resolved, you can easily move on to the next.

Hardy people are involved and dedicated; they are completely in command of their lives and change is not perceived as a threat but as a chance for improvement. Hardy personalities are less likely to fall ill than highly stressed people who feel powerless and unable to cope, have an aversion to change, and see security as the status quo. Hardy personalities are to be envied and in Part Two, you will find strategies to help you become 'hardy' and resistant to stress.

Chapter Four

The Health Hazards of Stress

Muscular tension, headaches, tightness in the chest – these are the classic initial reactions to negative stress that most of us have experienced at one time or another. But have you ever wondered why you experience them? Why it is that when you are going for a job interview your body seems to rebel. Your palms become sweaty and damp; butterflies – or is it elephants? – seem to stampede in your tummy, disrupting your concentration; and your heart rate increases to such an alarming height you can feel it pounding in your chest. And, of course, the more you worry about your sweaty palms and butterfly tummy, the worse they get.

These stress reactions may seem untimely and inconvenient but they do in fact serve a necessary purpose. The body has its own protective mechanism for dealing with any occurrences that put a strain on it. And the underlying purpose of every stress reaction is to maintain the body's integral balance. Under stress, your body has to function in a different way in order to maintain the status quo.

The stages of stress Stressful situations trigger a chain reaction in the body. For example, if you are suddenly scared by a noise in the middle of the night, your body instantaneously reacts with the 'flight or fight' reaction. When you realize that it is just the dustbin lid blowing over, your body quickly reverts to its normal balanced state. The smaller the event, the easier it is for this rebalancing process to take place.

In the inconsequential example of the crashing dustbin lid, there is only one recognizable stage of stress – alarm. However, in more profound stressful situations, there are in fact three recognizable stages:

- the alarm phase;
- the resistance phase;
- and the exhaustion phase.

The alarm phase

Our bodies enter the alarm phase whenever we are faced with a stressful situation, be it jumping out of the way of a car or confronting the managing director about a pay increase. The basic purpose of this stage is to prepare the body for immediate action: energy is mobilized to cope with the emergency, real or imagined, and your physical capabilities are heightened for speed or power *(see diagram on page 34)*. The alarm phase blocks out everything except for what is immediately needed to deal with the situation. In this first stage of stress the rush of adrenaline may give you an intense feeling of excitement and you may feel sharper and more alert.

Perhaps paradoxically, the alarm phase does not have to start and finish in a flash – it can last for several hours or even longer than a day. But at the start of the alarm phase there is always an end in sight. In other words, you are able to foresee that, when all the excitement is over, you will be able to relax.

Fiona, a 26-year-old publicity manager for a publishing company, had to take over the organization of the end-of-year sales conference at the last minute when her boss fell ill. Despite the enormity of the task her body's instinctive response was able to help her. A rush of adrenaline gave her a 'buzz' and she felt razor sharp and ready for anything. She also found that she needed less sleep, was able to make quick decisions when needed, and she also had bags of energy. Not surprisingly, she got the job done.

The following are classic signs that indicate the alarm phase:

• speeding up of all activity;
• you feel under pressure of time;
• you feel as if you are being driven (which, of course, you are by the activating system);
• a feeling of 'I want to...' spurs you on.

What happens to your body during stress

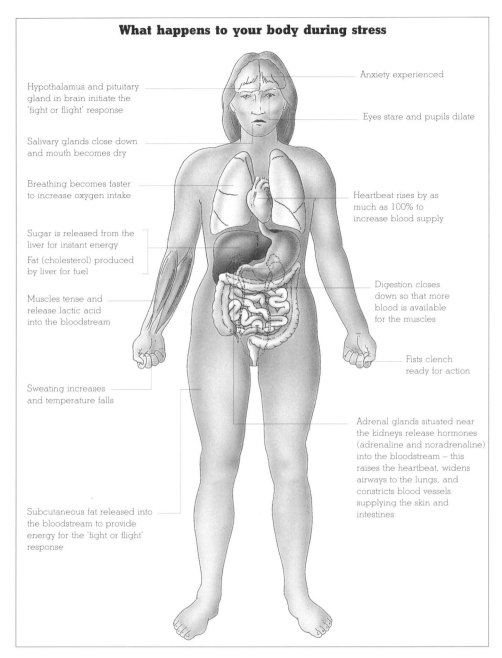

Hypothalamus and pituitary gland in brain initiate the 'fight or flight' response

Anxiety experienced

Eyes stare and pupils dilate

Salivary glands close down and mouth becomes dry

Breathing becomes faster to increase oxygen intake

Heartbeat rises by as much as 100% to increase blood supply

Sugar is released from the liver for instant energy

Fat (cholesterol) produced by liver for fuel

Muscles tense and release lactic acid into the bloodstream

Digestion closes down so that more blood is available for the muscles

Fists clench ready for action

Sweating increases and temperature falls

Adrenal glands situated near the kidneys release hormones (adrenaline and noradrenaline) into the bloodstream – this raises the heartbeat, widens airways to the lungs, and constricts blood vessels supplying the skin and intestines

Subcutaneous fat released into the bloodstream to provide energy for the 'fight or flight' response

At the end of the alarm stage, when the stressful situation is over, the body can return to normal. Provided there is time to relax before the next challenge, this type of stress is good for you and is stimulating. There should be no long-lasting ill effects.

If, however, the stress factors continue or if there is an ongoing series of crises in your life, the stress responses will be kept switched on and you may move on to the next phase.

If you experience a continuous series of stressors, or one crisis after another, your body has to make provision for a longer term protection.

The resistance phase

Joan, a 45-year-old personnel manager, was experiencing difficulties at work with the arrival of a new boss who seemed hell-bent on making changes just for the sake of it. Her teenage sons were, for the first time, constantly in trouble at school and her mother had recently had a fall. Her mother's injuries were minor but the accident left her feeling frail and frightened which meant that she needed more help to get about. Joan, of course, was the only person her mother wanted. The situation continued for months, with Joan trying to please everyone. Not surprisingly, she began to feel trapped.

This kind of prolonged stress is common for many people – you may recognize it as being similar to your own. In this kind of situation there may be no clear course of action to take nor any obvious way of resolving things. In such circumstances there is little or no time for your body to return to its normal state of relaxation and the chain reaction does not have time to subside. In fact, the reverse tends to happen – the effects of stress snowball and get worse rather than better. The result is that your energy stores get run down as you struggle to meet everyone's demands; mentally and physically, you steadily grow weaker as the pressures get greater.

Danger signs of the resistance phase:

- bouts of irritation;
- overreaction to minor problems;
- an altered sleep pattern;
- an outburst of anger;
- a feeling of 'I have to...' or 'I can't escape...'

The resistance stage can leave you feeling depressed, listless, stripped of confidence, and with little or no idea of how to improve your situation. Thus, the phase becomes self-perpetuating.

If you recognize these signs in yourself, then the stress has gone on too long. It is time to stop and take stock of your life. If you carry on, you may simply drift into the third phase of stress – exhaustion.

The exhaustion phase If the stressful situations do not ease up, your body never gets a chance to rebalance itself and you finally become exhausted. At this stage, you start feeling really ill and you need to see a doctor. During the exhaustion phase, stress starts becoming obvious emotionally, physically and intellectually. In effect, your brain completely drains of energy.

> Peter, a 35-year-old financial adviser, found that months of putting in extra hours with no let up had finally taken their toll. He found it hard to get up in the morning and the same thoughts kept spinning around in his head. Despite all his hard work, everything seemed to be working against him – he now felt less confident than when he first started the job and the smallest task seemed insurmountable. Even colleagues had commented that, 'He didn't seem to be his old self.'

In the exhaustion phase, the tired mind is only capable of dealing with mundane matters at a low level. It is also the phase during which errors and dangerous accidents can happen.

Some obvious danger signs that indicate the exhaustion phase:

- recurring headaches;
- palpitations and chest pains;
- inability to concentrate;
- frequently feeling unable to cope;
- insomnia;
- emotional shut down, except for anger and frustration;
- burnout.

The exhaustion phase of stress, during which mind and body effectively grind to a halt, is sometimes very aptly described as 'burnout'. The only cure for burnout is complete rest, sleep and a period of doing absolutely nothing.

If you feel that you could be at breaking point, the questionnaire on page 38 will help you find how near you are to burning out. If you score ten Ts or more, you could be well on the way.

Performance improves as arousal increases but there comes a point where fatigue sets in. This is followed by a slump in performance and exhaustion. Ultimately, the decline can lead to ill health and total breakdown.

The human function curve

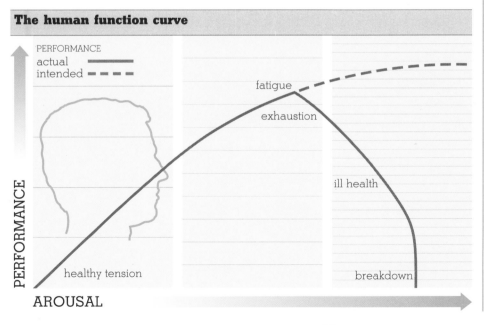

PERFORMANCE
actual ━━━━━
intended ▬ ▬ ▬ ▬

fatigue

exhaustion

ill health

healthy tension

breakdown

PERFORMANCE

AROUSAL

Against each statement write T if it is mostly true or F if it is mostly false. Count up how many Ts you have scored. If you have ten or more you may be on the way to burnout.

Are you burning out?

I feel emotionally exhausted	
I have recently lost my sense of humour	
I experience shortness of breath	
I am reluctant to take time off work for holidays	
I frequently feel irritable	
I don't feel like talking to people	
It takes me longer to get things done than usual	
I feel trapped	
I have difficulty sleeping	
I am more critical than usual	
I do not have time to stop for lunch	
I find it difficult to switch off and relax	
I frequently have physical symptoms such as muscle tension and digestive problems	
I feel more suspicious than usual	
I don't have any time for myself	
I frequently work 10-hour days	
I constantly feel tired and worn out	
I am drinking more alcohol than usual	
I frequently feel frustrated	
I have lost interest in my work	

With short-term stress, there is an end, a period during which it is possible to unwind, collect thoughts and get back to normal. With long-term stress, there is no apparent end and, like an overwrought computer, the brain starts to pack up under the continuous onslaught of strain. Burnout is the body's way of saying STOP but there is no predicting exactly when the moment is going to arrive. All you can do is take account of stress levels and try to prevent burnout from happening – if you ignore the preliminary symptoms, the consequences can be dangerous. However, having said that, it is all too easy to get swept up in a tide of events that carry you to the breaking point and it is often not easy to take control. Here is a hypothetical example of how a person could get carried to snapping point through no fault of his own and without even realizing it.

Short-term and long-term stress

Short-term stress

Jim, a 50-year-old manager of a printing company, arrives at work knowing that he has an important meeting to attend with his superiors to discuss his performance. The meeting goes better than he had anticipated and he goes away happy with what was said. He has time to relax before returning to his normal work routine and his body has time to regain its normal balance without any ill effects.

Long-term stress

One outcome of Jim's performance review is that he is relocated to a bigger site. He now has to commute an hour each way to work, driving across a busy town. Before, he had a 15-minute journey and that was on a bad day. But that is not the only new stressor he has to face. Shortly after the move, Jim has a meeting with his new superiors which does not go well and his performance is criticized. His new workload is strange to him and he finds it hard to concentrate as he is constantly interrupted. He rarely finds time to take a decent break and one day the computer crashes and he loses hours of work. Nothing seems to go right.

Burnout

Jim's life repeats the above pattern for a period of several months. His work is constantly criticized and so he puts in longer hours trying to turn things around. As he gets more and more worn down, he becomes withdrawn. He feels and fears failure. He starts to avoid his colleagues and is reluctant to communicate with anyone, including his wife. He begins taking time off for a variety of ailments and his isolation grows. He is worried about the prospect of redundancy and feels unable to cope. He is reaching burnout stage.

Stress and illness

By now you will be acquainted with the symptoms of stress and should have an idea of what stage of stress you are at. During the alarm phase there is little impact on health providing the body has time to return to normal once the stress situation has been dealt with. However, if stress is experienced over a long period of time, then illness is a realistic possibility long before the burnout stage.

Everyone responds differently to stress situations and everybody has a different threshold as to how much stress they can take before becoming ill. Some can survive the most amazing stresses for long periods – as seen in prisoner of war camps, for example – but others succumb sooner. The relevance of stress regarding the onset of illness depends on the severity and duration of the stressors and on your own vulnerability.

Most people have weak spots, and it is these which will be the first to give way to pressure. The nature of the weak spots will play a large part in determining whether constant stress results in a minor or major illness. Alcoholism, depression, persistent diarrhoea, impotence, menstrual disorders, migraine, psoriasis, and intestinal ulcers are just a few of the illnesses that are often related to stress.

Take the time to reflect on your own health for a moment or two – it could be that minor illnesses that you just take for granted are in fact stress-related. Do you get colds that you cannot to shake off, or are you ever plagued by bouts of constipation? If so, do they coincide with stressful times in your life? Make a list of any illnesses that you have had recently and then try to remember what the major stress factors were in your life at the time. It is also worthwhile noting in a diary recurring health problems that you are aware of – persistent headaches or neckaches, for example. Against this list write down events that might have caused your symptoms. The longer you keep the diary, the more comprehensive the overall picture will be.

Prevention is better than cure so it pays to learn how to manage your stress in a positive way so that you can prevent stress-related illnesses and diseases creeping up on you. In Part Two you will learn how to adapt your lifestyle and behaviour to improve your health and general wellbeing.

Diary record of health/stress

September 17
Diarrhoea

Sleepless night worrying about competence test

September 19
Neckache all afternoon

I could throttle Jo-jo at work – she makes me mad

September 22
Feel really down

Baby cried all last night

September 23
Diarrhoea (again!)

Results of test due

September 25
Depressed and twitchy

Baby teething – he finds it hard to sleep

September 29
Bad neckache

Jo-jo at it again first thing on Monday morning

Chapter Five

How Do You Cope with Stress at the Moment?

Life in the twentieth century throws up stressors from almost every quarter. While there is often little we can do to avoid them completely, we can adapt our lifestyles to help us withstand their negative effects. Eating and drinking habits, whether or not we exercise, our sleeping patterns – such things as these can help or hinder our ability to cope with stress both in the short-term but, most especially, in the long-term.

Take a long, hard look at yourself. Do you sometimes drink to cheer yourself up or to help you forget the row you had with your boss? Do you ever take drugs to help you sleep? Do you smoke incessantly? Do you bottle up your feelings? Do you purposefully avoid difficult situations? Do you ever refuse to open statements from your bank or credit card company? These are all all classic signs that stress is having a negative effect.

These are by no means the only symptoms of stress but if any of them ring a bell with you, it could be that your lifestyle is actually making things more difficult rather than easier. A drink, a smoke, a pill – all these offer, usually unsuccessfully, is a short-term remedy. Would it not be better to change your lifestyle so that you did not suffer so much?

If you are stressed and constantly ignore your lifestyle, the chances are that one day, stress will get the better of you. By making time for yourself and adopting healthy lifestyle habits you will increase your ability to cope with everyday hiccoughs that might otherwise create anxiety. It might sound obvious but it is astonishing how many people ignore the self-evident and carry on regardless! Regular exercise, a well balanced diet made up of wholefood and plenty of fresh fruit and vegetables, combined with quiet times for relaxation, will provide you with the armoury you need to deal with the daily onslaught of frustration and tension.

You may think that you are locked into a lifestyle that you cannot change significantly. This is rarely true and most of us can adapt or alter our lifestyles to enable us to cope with stress in the long-term so that life's minor wrinkles do not bother us unduly. First, however, it is important to acknowledge those things that you do – or do not do – at the moment which could help you and your body deal with daily stressful situations. Complete the questionnaire to find out.

You and your coping resources

The factors in the chart below have been found to enhance people's ability to deal with stress. Tick Yes or No to each statement.

You and your coping resources

Stressor	Yes	No
I eat one good, hot, balanced meal per day		
At least four days per week, I get seven to eight hours sleep per night		
I give and receive affection regularly		
I have at least one relative within a few miles on whom I can rely		
I exercise to the point of exertion about two times per week		
I do not smoke		
I do not drink alcohol to excess		
I am the right weight for my height and age		
I have an income adequate to meet basic expenses		
I regularly attend church		
I regularly attend club or social activities		
I have friends whom I see regularly		
I have a few friends I confide in about personal matters		
I am in good health (including eyesight, hearing and teeth)		
I am able to speak openly about my feelings		

You and your coping resources (cont.)

Stressor	Yes	No
I have regular conversations with people I live with about domestic issues, e.g. household chores, money.		
I do something for fun at least once per week.		
I am able to organize my time effectively.		
I drink less than three cups of coffee (or tea or cola drinks) per day.		
I take a quiet time for myself each day.		

If you have more Nos than Yeses, your lifestyle is doing little to help you deal with stress. If anything, it could be increasing your vulnerability to stress. The best thing you can do is turn to Chapter Fifteen in Part Two where you will find exercises to help you restore balance and harmony to your life. Taking action demands some determination on your part but the effort is well worthwhile and within a short space of time you will be rewarded by actually seeing and feeling the positive results. If you take action and repeat the questionnaire in three month's time, you should discover that you have more Yeses than Nos.

Chapter Six

Feel Good about Yourself

By now you will be aware that stress is something that you create – it is your response to stressful situations. So, for an event to be stressful, much depends how you view that event and how you feel about yourself. For example, most people have a dread of examinations, but if you are able to walk into an examination hall feeling positive – perhaps because you passed an important examination when you were young – you can actually relish the stress which gives you a head start over the rest. This so called 'feel-good factor' is central to how you handle new and challenging situations – meeting new people, learning new skills or performing under pressure – with greater confidence and less negative stress.

Believing in yourself helps you become more resilient to stress. It shapes your attitude towards life. It enables you to feel positive about getting through difficult situations and about your life generally. This confidence, in turn, will often encourage you to seek out new challenges – and as a result you will achieve more in life.

Conversely, self-doubt can eat away inside you without you realizing what you are doing to yourself. Self-doubt can sabotage your actions. Worse still, your colleagues, your boss or even a prospective new employer may recognize that you are not one hundred per cent sure of yourself and may not offer you new opportunities as a result. If you constantly doubt the quality of your work, it will encourage others to question your abilities, too.

If you lack self-confidence, work is by no means the only aspect of your life that can suffer either. It can deplete your social skills and the way potential partners see you – at worse they may not ask you out or accept your offer of a date. Similarly, if you doubt your ability to win in competition, your opponent will pick this up and turn it to his or her advantage by increasing the pressure.

PART TWO

HOW TO CONTROL STRESS

The good news is that self-doubt does not have to rule your life. It is not difficult to develop effective strategies to boost your self-image and you can easily learn how to feel good about yourself, and, above all, believe in yourself.

Improve your self-image

Most of us can benefit from improving our self-image. Carry out the exercises suggested in this chapter and you can give yourself a confidence boost – they can unquestionably help to speed you on your way to your goals.

Practise your skills

You need to be aware of weaknesses in your skills. For example, do you work on a computer but cannot use the latest software that would make your job easier? If so, you could be making yourself feel inadequate or incompetent.

Once you have recognized your weak points, set about trying to improve them. This will boost your overall confidence. Spend some time writing down your weak spots and make a plan of action to improve them. Do not expect everything to improve at once – allow a realistic time scale for your skills to improve and measure your progress. If time is of the essence, then work first on those skills that will help you achieve your goals and let go of the less important items.

Skills improvement list

Inadequate skill	How to improve
1. Hopeless cook – especially for impromptu dinner parties.	Watch TV chef every Thursday 7pm for ideas.
2. Baffled by latest computers at work – everyone else thinks they're wonderful!	Ask Sue (boss) for opportunities for day release course on computers OR check out evening classes.

Take a good look at yourself. Are you happy with what you see? Are you presenting an image, both to yourself and others, that says, 'I'm confident and happy about who and what I am?'

If not, check out your wardrobe and throw out the clothes that do not fit with that confident image. What about your hairstyle? Are your skin and nails in good condition? Looking good can help you to feel good and so avoid self-doubt.

Think about your posture. Do you slouch or walk tall? If you have tendency to walk along looking at your feet, try walking with your head up with your eyes aimed at the roof tops. This may seem silly, but psychologists have found that it much harder for you to experience negative feelings when you look upwards.

Polish your image

Another way to boost your self-image is to learn how to recognize those times when you perform well or deal effectively with a difficult situation. And when you do, give yourself and pat on the back – the chances are nobody else will.

Reward yourself

It is well known that people are generally quite poor at praising others. We tend to focus on people's faults, forgetting to say 'Well done' when credit is due. Develop ways of praising yourself and feel good about it when you do. It will then be easier to praise others. *(Also see Chapter Nine: Reducing Stress in Relationships.)*

Cast your mind back over the last year and you will probably find that you have made a lot of progress in many ways and in several different areas of your life that you have not really acknowledged. Now think about events that left you disappointed and try to find something positive about them by identifying what you learnt from the experience. It may have been hellish but what new knowledge did you gain that you can take forward with you into the future?

Acknowledging the good things in your life and realizing that you can learn an awful lot from the not-so-good, is another way of rewarding yourself and avoiding the stress that self-doubt brings.

Recognize your positive qualities

One of the symptoms of stress is that you forget to focus on positive qualities and skills – instead you get caught up in negative thoughts and emotions. You are particularly likely to do this when you feel over-whelmed or under pressure because that is when it is easiest to lose a sense of perspective.

A simple way to regain your control is mentally to step back from your environment and take a look at yourself to establish whether or not you have things in balance. Run over the events of the last week. Think about the tasks that you completed and identify the skills you used. You may take these for granted but, remember, not everyone can do the same things as you.

Take a piece of paper and list the skills that you have used in the last week. Your skills are activities that you do well or have a flair for, perhaps cooking, typing or chairing meetings. Think of the times when you have been praised or rewarded by others, it will help you to recognize your achievements.

On a second sheet of paper, list your positive qualities, the things that are special about you. You could perhaps include your friendly personality, or your ability to be positive in difficult circumstances.

Skills used during week

1. Computer skills – taught Fred how to use new software.
2. Patience – looked after neighbour's baby on Saturday.
3. Diplomacy – broke up argument between J and K.
4. Organization – arranged surprise birthday party for Bill.
5. Head for figures – sorted out Angie's financial problems.

Positive qualities

1. Affectionate
2. Witty (make others laugh)
3. Good with children
4. Friendly to strangers
5. Decisive

Once you have completed your lists stick them somewhere visible where you can read them and add to them regularly. Recognizing your positive qualities is an effective way to reduce the stress of negative thinking. It also puts you in touch with all the useful resources that you have for dealing with awkward or difficult situations when you are under pressure.

Confidence is all about knowing your capabilities. So it is important to build a positive memory bank of all the times that you have performed well.

Build your confidence

To build up your positive memory bank, you will need some quiet time. Relax in a favourite chair and mentally wander back through time, rather like going back through a calendar. As you do so, allow all your good performances to pop into your mind such as when people congratulated you, when you had a good work appraisal, or how proud you felt when your children graduated from college. First, spend the time just enjoying the memories, then write them down. Read your list regularly to boost your confidence.

A few last words on boosting confidence: try not to put yourself down. Everyone has successes in their life and now is the time to get better at recognizing yours.

We have already discussed the fact that the only person who creates negative stress is you. Most of us do this without thinking – we constantly berate ourselves with negative talk and make negative comments to ourselves such as, 'I'll never get this finished in time.'

Adopt stress-free self-talk

The danger of negative self-talk is that it can become self-fulfilling. Before you know it, you can end up believing the worst has happened or is about to happen. Mentally, you begin to rehearse failing and eventually that is what you do. Whenever you catch yourself doing this, try to reverse the process as successful, stress-free people do.

To feel good about yourself, to be successful and resilient to stress, start to send yourself positive messages. Tell yourself, 'I look good and feel great' or 'I will get this done.'

Chapter Seven

Change Your Thoughts

Our emotions and thoughts are closely linked. If you feel stressed you will probably find that you are acutely aware of your negative emotions and less aware of your logical thinking patterns. You may believe that it is a natural course of events to feel and think negatively when the pressure is on. Some people even believe that the way they feel is due to their personality – that they are 'born worriers'. But you will be pleased to learn that this is just not the case. To a large extent you can choose your emotions – you do not have to be controlled by them.

In this chapter, you will be shown how to identify where your emotions come from and you will learn strategies for changing them so that you will be more able to combat stress positively.

Previous conditioning A lot of behaviour is learnt and for most of us the chief point of reference is our parents. How your parents responded to pressured or difficult circumstances can explain a great deal about how you respond to similar situations.

Think about how your parents reacted to stressful situations when you were growing up. Were they anxious and fretful during uncertain times? Are you the same? You may also have grown up developing a host of beliefs that are 'irrational', such as the need for constant approval. You will be relieved to hear that there is much you can do to alleviate the negative stress caused by irrational beliefs and thoughts.

Approval seeking If your parents encouraged you to be good and behave well to please them, you may be still be seeking approval from others as feedback that you are doing well. Trying to do this as an adult can be very wearing on yourself and others. There may be times when you have to make unpopular decisions or take command of a difficult situation, and pleasing everyone involved would be neither possible nor appropriate. Managing people at work and managing family relationships are areas where this can apply.

Trying to please everyone can be stressful, even more so when no one seems to appreciate the efforts you are making on their behalf. It is also unrealistic to expect everyone to like you. Once you realize that that is what you have been doing, and once you decide to change your expectations, it becomes easier to function in a pressured environment and much of the stress of dealing with people and making unpopular decisions is removed.

Constantly trying to keep everyone happy can also be time-consuming and tiring. This kind of thinking is irrational and is loaded with problems. From the moment you learn someone does not approve of your actions, it can set up negative thoughts: you start to think that you are not good enough or that nobody likes you.

Strategies for change

- Think about the people whom you spend a lot of time trying to please unnecessarily or for too much of the time – your boss, for example, or your sister, or your partner – and re-evaluate your actions around them. *(Refer to Chapter Ten: Assert Yourself to improve your communication techniques.)*

- Identify the times when you have been oversensitive about other people criticizing you and start to build an acceptance that it is natural that there will be some people who may not approve of you.

Striving for perfection

How many times in your childhood was the phrase 'could do better' applied to you? Parents and teachers give us this feedback with the good intention of getting us to do our best. But they sometimes forget the most important part of the message: 'Well done, for what you have achieved so far.'

Without necessarily criticizing your parents or your teachers, this kind of upbringing may well have left you with ideals that are not always useful in pressured circumstances. If you have five important things to do in a short space of time, it is better to accept an adequate job for each of the five rather than exhaust yourself trying to achieve the impossible perfect result for all of them.

Strategy for change

- Keep a time-log diary for a week to monitor the time you are spending on ongoing activities. Then analyse your diary to assess how much time and effort you are giving to each activity. If you are feeling stressed because of the energy you have put in to complete each task to an impeccable standard, be bold and plan a new schedule for the following week that will allow you to go a bit easier on yourself.

Blaming others for unhappiness

You may have grown up with very caring parents who wanted to protect you from experiencing difficulties. Perhaps they shielded you from stressful situations such as being bullied or teased. Perhaps your parents even fought your battles for you in order for you to feel happy most of the time.

If this is the case, you will not have developed your own coping strategies and you may tend to blame others for any stress you experience. If, for example, there are changes at the office which result in you having to do more work, you might blame your boss because you feel stressed. Or, perhaps your partner has to relocate and you blame him or her for the emotional upheaval.

Blaming others when things go wrong means you are not taking responsibility for yourself. In time, this kind of thinking can leave you feeling helpless and unable to do anything for yourself. To blame others for your apparent misfortunes is, in effect, an easy option and 'passing the buck' is never satisfactory in the long-term. And, if you always point the finger at someone else whenever anything goes wrong, the chances are that they will not give you support when you most genuinely need it. In other words, you could find yourself increasingly isolated from work colleagues or even members of your immediate family.

Claire's partner, Mark, is a successful civil engineer. He loves his job but it is one that takes him out of the country for half of the year. Claire misses him terribly when he is away, so much so when Mark is at home their time together is marred with arguments about how lonely she feels.

When Claire came to see me their relationship was at crisis point. In the course of time, however, she began to realize that neither Mark nor his job were to blame for the emptiness of her life and, if anything, she was at fault for transferring the responsibility for her unhappiness on to him. Claire has since joined an amateur dramatic society which fills in the time when Mark is away and which has also proved to be a good source of new friends.

Strategy for change

• Think about the stress you are experiencing at the moment. What is causing it? Are you blaming everyone but yourself? If so, decide to take responsibility for your own actions and feelings and manage them differently. When you do take responsibility for your behaviour and actions, you will probably be relieved to discover that your whole outlook on life becomes more positive.

Faulty thinking patterns

There are certain ways in which we think – thinking patterns – that can sometimes give us a biased view of our environment. This bias can become more noticeable, and more destructive, in some people when they are stressed. Outlined below are some ways by which it is possible to change recognized thinking patterns for the better.

Over-generalization

Does it only need a couple of things to go wrong for your mind to make a quantum leap and imagine that *everything* is going wrong, that your life is caving in around you? This kind of response to stress is an over-generalized thinking pattern. And again, it is one that can be learned from parents. Did they fly off the handle when things went wrong or did they calmly take problems in their stride.

Hillary was the senior administrator for a large accountancy firm. In the year that she had been there, she had been allowed a free rein to do what she wanted. When the annual management review found that a couple of changes needed to be made, Hillary was astounded and upset. She began to feel that 'everything' at work was changing and she believed that she no longer enjoyed her work. She became so anxious about the changes that needed to be made that she decided that the only way round it was to begin looking for a new job, further adding to her stress.

Over-generalized thinking is stressful in itself but it becomes worse if, like Hillary, you make decisions on the back of it and instead of finding solutions for the few things that need changing, decide to move away from the environment altogether.

Strategy for change
- Separate out the aspects of your life that you find stressful from those that are working well. Write them down in two columns. How easy or difficult did you find this exercise? The harder you found it, the more likely it is that you are over-generalizing.

Aspects of life list

Working well	Stressful
Love life	Demands of work
Relationship with L (boss)	Competition between colleagues
Friendship with P and S	Health (backache in particular)
Financial rewards	Not enough time with children
Meeting new and interesting people all the time at work	

You might find it easier to look at specific aspects of your life – for example, relationships, leisure activities, staying healthy, and working life. When you have completed the lists, you will discover that your life is not all gloom and despondency and have a clearer picture of what is good. In the future, do not ignore the good bits!

Focusing on one particular part of a whole picture can be a sign of selective thinking and this can be as negative as over-generalizing. If all you concentrate on is one task or event, then everything else is ignored, often to your detriment – that task or event dominates your thinking to such an extent that anxiety, worry and fatigue are bound to follow.

Selective thinking

Sally's local school was holding a charity softball game. There would also be stalls selling home-made cakes and preserves, and a clown show to keep the children happy during the game. Despite all the things that were happening during the day, all Sally could think of was the teas she had to make. Because that was all she could think about the teas eventually became a source of stress and ruined her whole day.

• Think about an event or occasion that you find stressful and notice whether or not you have one recurring thought or whether a wider range of considerations come to your mind. If you tend to have the former, then you are selectively thinking. Start to broaden your thinking by taking account of other things. This will help you keep everything in a healthy perspective.

Strategy for change

A negative outlook on the circumstances and events in your life can make you feel worried, guilty and can even destroy your self-confidence. Remaining positive when situations seem to be conspiring against you can be difficult but being positive does help you to retain feelings of being in control. Being able to change a negative thought into a positive one is an important stress management technique.

Negative thinking

55

Strategies for change

- Make a list of the recurring negative thoughts that enter your mind. You might find it helpful to start by making a list of the negative emotions that you are aware of and then identifying the thinking behind them. For example, if you feel depressed at work, it may be due to you thinking that you are inadequate because you are so busy you cannot do your job properly.

Now read back over your list. Think about each item carefully and change it to a more acceptable, positive statement. For instance, you might say, 'I am good enough and I can do my job effectively.'

- Affirmations – simple statements that you repeat to yourself – provide an effective way of reprogramming yourself to think positively. One famous affirmation made by the French pioneer of auto-suggestion, Emile Coué, is, 'Every day, in every way, I am becoming better and better,' but there is no reason why you should not make up an affirmation which you think is especially appropriate for you. You could say, 'The more I learn, the more I understand' or even just, 'I am a good person.' Repeat the positive statement you create every day when you wake up and before you go to bed. Affirmations work, but only as a gradual process so do not expect dramatic changes overnight.

- Negative thinking can affect how you deal with particularly stressful situations that you have to experience in your life on a one-off or regular basis. The emotional turmoil created by these situations can be very debilitating and can, over a period of time, develop into a phobia. 'Desensitization' is an effective technique that helps to reduce the impact such events have on you. Here is how to use it.

Focus on a situation that is or has been particularly stressful for you, a business meeting, for example. Write down an account of the event from start to finish. Include as much detail as you can and be as descriptive as possible. If commuting is stressful for you then your list might look a little this.

Desensitization – commuting

- *I feel panicky as I approach the station.*
- *My breathing becomes shallow as I buy my ticket.*
- *I feel fearful just standing on the crowded platform.*
- *My fear intensifies as I hear the train approach and I worry about being pushed off the platform.*
- *My heart pounds as I get on the train.*
- *Standing in the crowded compartment makes me feel breathless and I feel dizzy when the train stops in tunnels.*
- *By the time I get to work I feel positively exhausted.*

Once you have written down every element of your stressful situation, rank each statement according to how stressful it feels. Start with 1 being the least stressful. Rewrite your list in rank order, starting with number 1.

Now sit somewhere quiet. If you feel tense, use the relaxation CD *(see Chapter Twelve)* to help you unwind. Really try to become aware of your body as the tension slips away and, as you start to relax, pay attention to the depth of your breathing. When you are feeling comfortable and easy, think about the first item on your list. As you do, hold on to that feeling of relaxation. If you feel the slightest bit of stress creeping in, let the thought go; try to re-establish your initial feeling of relaxation. If necessary, listen to the CD again and try running over the first point on your list once more – it could take a number of attempts to remain relaxed while thinking about the first point, so do not give up.

Once you have mastered point number 1, move on to number 2. As before, the object is to remain relaxed while thinking about the stressful situation. Repeat the procedure until you can remain calm and relaxed while thinking about points 1 and 2.

Practise this technique over the next few days or weeks until you are able to relive the whole scene in your mind while remaining relaxed.

The next step is put the sense of relaxation into practice for real. Relax yourself before confronting the situation and try to regain the feeling of peace whenever you feel yourself beginning to panic. If you do begin to feel panicky, deepen your breathing and push your abdomen out when you breathe in – this simple breathing exercise can be a great help as it removes stomach tension.

- Visualization, which is sometimes called visual imagination, is another useful way of dealing with negative thoughts. Unpleasant memories of an event that went disastrously wrong in the past can make similar occasions in the present stressful. For example, if every time you have to present the monthly sales figures reminds you of the time when you had to present a project at school and everyone, including the teacher, laughed at you, the chances are you will find presentations particularly stressful occasions. Before you know it you are sweating and your mouth has dried up, making the presentation even more difficult. In a situation like this, visualization can help.

Start by recalling the unpleasant memory. Keep it in your mind and really focus on the scene. Then begin to change the image. Try making the picture bigger or smaller – there will come a time when the scene looks so totally ridiculous, it may even make you laugh. Imagine that you are using the zoom lens on a camera to send your picture off into the distance or to bring it up close – distant images tend to weaken distressing feelings. Now turn your picture into bright colours, then hazy grey images – this can also help to weaken negative feelings.

Finding ways to change negative memories can help to lessen the impact that they have on your life at present – you cannot change events from your past but you can reduce their damaging, long-lasting effects. Keep working on these images and you will increase the control that you have over your emotions.

Chapter Eight

Learn to Cope with Change

Some people can cope with change better than others but there are certain life changes that are stressful for everybody. Look back at the Holmes and Rahe table you completed on pages 16–17. Your total is an indication of how much change you have gone through in the last year. If you scored highly, it follows that you have experienced a lot of very significant change in your life recently.

This is not uncommon. People are now experiencing changes in more than just one part of their lives as a result of much bigger changes going on in the world. Environmental changes like global warming have added the worry of skin cancer to the daily lives of people living in hot climates. Competition between companies is greater which means big businesses have to respond to market demands much quicker than in the past. Changes in technology mean that communication is faster and more effective, so we learn news of other countries quickly and can mobilize an equally rapid response. With technology have come portable phones and computers which allow us to work from home or while travelling large distances from our offices. Families have had to become more mobile and have to be prepared to relocate. More people work to short contracts or are self-employed and the notion of a job for life has all but disappeared. The idea of an upwardly mobile career is disappearing, too, as people recognize that they may have a number of different jobs and may have to develop different skills throughout their lifetimes. No doubt you will be able to think of many more changes that could be influencing you.

Any change brings with it a degree of uncertainty. And because we lack information about the future, we tend to deal with it by holding on to what we know of the past in order to make sense of it. We do this in a number of stages. We may look on the dark side of the picture and become anxious and panicky about what might lie in store. We may also try to surmise about the future by talking to friends, colleagues and family about their expectations. This can create a grapevine effect whereby rumour, which we all know is frequently inaccurate, is passed round creating further anxiety to everyone concerned.

Developing strategies for coping with stress is vital if we are not to be left feeling overwhelmed by the tiniest change to our routine. One of the most effective techniques is to become familiar with these stages we go through when facing change. This will put you in a better position to manage change effectively for yourself and feel good about it as you do so.

How to manage change

In the course of my work I have found that the people who expect change, manage it best. Because they accept change as an ongoing natural part of life they tend of have a positive attitude towards it and hence better coping strategies. They read the signs that change is coming, learn to interpret what they mean, and are consequently better able to cope when it happens. Treating change as a challenge empowers you. It lets you remain in control of the circumstances within it. As a result, any associated stress is kept to a bare minimum.

Get used to thinking about change and start to expect it in your life. Look at your future. What do you hope to achieve in the next five or ten years? It is a question that most of us only think about when we are going to job interviews. But your life is more than your career and no doubt you will have goals that you will want to achieve outside your job.

Use this information to assess what changes you may have to make at work or at home. Prepare yourself mentally and start by taking small steps that will help you realize your goals. If you know that there are going to be major changes at work, start keeping an eye on job advertisements and also keep yourself informed about what changes any rival companies might be making.

The easiest way to avoid facing up to change is to deny it is happening.

Take your head out of the sand

Gary was a manager of a busy clothing store. He loved his job and could not imagine working anywhere else. Unfortunately, he had failed to pick up on the signals that head office wanted to relocate key members of staff, including him. Although he was given six months' notice, two weeks before the move Gary had still to find somewhere for his family to live. Gary was in what counsellors call 'denial'.

People in denial tend to carry on as normal, as if nothing has nor will change. Ultimately, when they are forced to face up to reality, it can be very stressful. Suddenly, they have a million and one things do and they feel overwhelmed by the task ahead. They also carry the extra burden of having to function normally while still feeling the shock of finally waking up to the inevitable. Do you tend to say thing like, 'It will never happen to me' or 'They would never do that to me.' Both are typical denial statements.

As a counsellor I have worked with many people who have made similar comments about their job situation. They came to me feeling stressed because they suddenly found their jobs had been made redundant. Other people in the company had seen the signs and had been preparing for the worst by keeping an eye on the job market. As a result those people were in a stronger position when the 'unthinkable' happened.

Remember, though, that gossip on the grapevine can create alarm. In order to prepare for change you need to be confident that the information is accurate before you make a decision. Planning for change on the strength of hearsay can be just as stressful as denying it will ever happen.

First you need to assess whether some kind of change is certain, only a possibility, or just a figment of someone's imagination. Get information from the people that count – those who are authorities on the situation or who are decision makers. If it is difficult to talk in the office, invite them for a cup of coffee or a drink after work.

Also be aware that even the decision makers can change their minds. While they may tell you one thing, last minute developments could mean things go in the opposite direction!

Acceptance not resistance

Once you know that a change is going to happen, accept it and assess what impact, if any, it will have on your life. Ask yourself what good could come out of it for you. Identify what might be a downside and start to plan how to manage it. This will help you to maintain a feeling of control over the change and consequently the effect it has on your emotions.

Change inevitably results in you entering unknown territory. It can induce a whole range of emotions – fear, feelings of failure, a sense of isolation, and a general panic about coping. These are all perfectly understandable feelings but if you are unaware of this fact, you may find that you resist change by trying to hold on to old ways of doing things; you may even sabotage new methods and ideas.

If, say, your partner suggests that you fit a new burglar alarm on the house and you reply, 'It will never work' and then proceed to demonstrate exactly how it will fail, you would be showing a classic form of resistance to change, albeit a very simple one. Resistance can use up much needed energy reserves and also reduce the effectiveness of the transition. To say nothing of turning up the heat on your stress levels.

If you think you are resistant to change, try to alter your behaviour by identifying possible future changes to your life. Draw up a list and examine your attitude towards these new areas. Now what happens if you say to yourself, 'I can be curious about these new experiences?' Curiosity is an interesting state as it opens the mind to new possibilities and allows you to be creative in finding solutions to perceived problems. Go ahead and try it.

Look back on major or difficult changes that you have experienced in your life – leaving home for the first time, starting secondary school, moving house, getting married, or changing jobs. Reflect on how you felt before going into each event and how you felt after it was all over.

Turn a threat into a challenge

You will probably find that you worried about a lot of things that never actually happened. Perhaps you did not recognize the enjoyable parts of the experience such as making new friends, exploring ideas, or discovering new activities.

Apply the same technique to the changes you are facing at present: identify the feelings that you have currently and then imagine yourself coming out the other side, three months down the road. Eventually, make a list of the new opportunities and enjoyable experiences you have had that came as a result of the change.

Now that you can see that change can bring positive opportunities, turn your current feelings into more optimistic ones, safe in the knowledge that some good and enjoyable experiences lie ahead of you.

It can be stressful to try to hold on to old routines at the same time as developing new ways of operating. I have worked with people who have been told that their job has changed, that they no longer have to do certain tasks and others have priority. They have found it difficult to make the changes because of their attachment to the original tasks and have consequently overburdened themselves by trying to do it all. They have invariably blamed their bosses for causing their stress when, in fact, it was their inability to let go of old ways of doing things which caused their problems.

Goodbye to the old, hello to the new

Find ways to let go of old habits, territories or friendships. It can help to create a space in your mind for the 'new'. Having a leaving party, throwing out old files and training manuals – these are ways of discarding the old in favour of the new. Imagine being free from certain activities in your life – not everything 'old' is necessarily good!

Travel with ease through transition

Once the process of change has got under way, unfortunately you are still not in the clear! Accepting change is one thing, how you handle it is another.

Often when you let go of the 'old' and while you are exploring the new, the temptation is to try to do too much with the result that you turn into a 'headless chicken'. Running around creating too much to do in too little time, will be just as stressful as denial or even resisting change.

Coping successfully with change is all about staying in control. Once you feel committed to the change that you are experiencing – changing your job, moving to a new area or whatever – write down a list of things that have to be done. Set yourself short-term objectives to help you get through the initial stages and prioritise these items. *(Also see Chapter Eleven: Instant Ways To Manage Your Time.)*

Do not try to be a superwoman or superman to impress people with your effectiveness in your new role or environment. The chances are that if you try to do too much too quickly, you will make mistakes. You will gain far more from a steadier approach.

The right attitude

Facing change and travelling through transition can be managed effectively with the right attitude and with careful self-management. But how do you know if you have the right attitude? The following exercise will help you to assess your strengths and weaknesses for approaching change.

Think of a previous change in your circumstances that you have been through from start to finish. How did you manage each stage? Identify aspects that you could have improved and run through them again as you would have liked them to be.

Now list those new strategies. Read through them and make your thinking very positive by injecting positive statements such as, 'I can really enjoy going through changes,' or 'New and challenging experiences can come out of transitions.' Keep hold of this list and use it as a reference to help you get through future changes with the minimum of stress.

Chapter Nine

Reducing Stress in Relationships

The relationships you have with friends, a partner, or colleagues at work can be sources of support to help you get through difficult times. Alternatively, they can be sources of stress. In this chapter we will be looking at how to get the best out of your relationships.

Getting the support you need

No matter how resilient we think we are, everyone, at some time or another, needs the positive support of others to help them survive stressful times – the support we get from friends and family can be a substantial buffer against emotional strains. When dealing with any crisis – such as the death of a loved one, financial difficulty, or any situation which leaves you feeling unable to cope – remember that you do not have to face it alone. One of the vital things you need to do is to get help and support.

Express your feelings

The key to getting support is learning how to express your feelings. Try to avoid the 'stiff upper lip' approach to your problems, believing that if you ignore them for long enough they will go away. They usually do not. In truth, bottling up feelings invariably has the opposite affect – more often than not, bottling up makes problems seem worse than they are. Over a long period, containing your feelings can jeopardize your immune system and lead to illness. *(See Chapter Four: The Health Hazards Of Stress.)*

Believe it or not, there are many people out there just waiting to give you the support you need. First, however, you need to invite them in – it is up to you. Even if your family and friends are not close at hand, there is no reason to feel lonely and isolated. If you need help, it is important that you ask for it – it could be as simple as writing a letter or making a telephone call.

Making the first move

Asking for help may seem like an insurmountable task, a terrifying admission of failure. It is neither of those things. Think of it another way: if you avoid asking for help, you will have failed yourself and maybe others as well. Do not be afraid to make the first move and set yourself clear goals – create an ask-for-help action plan to help you take the first step:

- Make a list of positive-thinking people, whom you respect and whose opinion you value. Then make a conscious effort to see more of them.
- Invite a friend or member of your family, to whom you are close, to lunch to talk over your problems.
- If you do not have a network of friends, try to speak to at least one new person a week.
- Join a self-help group, evening class or voluntary activity organization – these provide meeting places for nurturing new friendships.
- Do not be afraid to seek professional help. If those you would normally discuss your problems with are too closely involved, then an impartial adviser – your doctor, a counsellor or a therapist – may be the answer to your problems.

Taking the stress out of relationships

Although the support of friends and family can be a lifeline for coping with stress, managing those relationships can be a source of stress, too. Most of us, at some time in our lives, have experienced difficult relationships. Professionally, this could be an uncooperative boss or colleague with whom you cannot get on; at home it could be the fact that your sister is still borrowing your clothes even though she is thirty!

Within families, tensions can arise almost out of nowhere – perhaps your husband constantly spends too long in the bathroom or your daughter is suddenly getting poor grades at school and is mixing with the wrong kids. Arguments can even flare up over which programme to watch on television or who has command of the remote control. The day-to-day momentum of any relationship has the potential for creating misunderstandings. So much so, that it is often the minor incidents that wear you down or cause you to blow your top. The trick in handling them effectively is to deal with them as soon as possible. The old adage that you should never go to sleep on an argument may not always be practical, but the message is clear.

Good relationships cannot be created instantly – they need to be fostered to preserve them and help them grow. Consequently, it is important to deal swiftly with the stress that they inevitably create. The following strategies will help you to take the stress out of relationships and, importantly, avoid misunderstandings. Used on a regular basis, these suggestions will help to prevent tension building up to pressure cooker levels.

The dos and don'ts in relationships

- Get to know yourself. To create good relationships, it helps to be comfortable with yourself. Inner conflict, brought on, say, by doing a job that you dislike, can make it difficult for you to strike a balance with others as your negative feelings may spill over into your work or home life.

Know yourself

It is important to take time off to understand what it is that is bringing on those negative feelings and to get the support that you need to help you make changes in your life. By identifying your strengths and weaknesses, by establishing your own goals and by recognizing your own values, you will be in a much better position to take control of your life and be far better equipped to manage your relationships.

- Do not expect too much from one relationship. Our thoughts and expectations often come from what we are taught as children. Relationships – both platonic and intimate – bring together people with different expectations, needs, and interpretations of what is 'right' or 'wrong'. Stress within a relationship is usually caused by a perceived failure of one person to fulfil another's needs – in effect, the two worlds collide with each other.

Realistic expectations

To avoid the collision, you must have realistic expectations of those involved in your life. It is unrealistic to expect one relationship to fulfil all your needs. It is a tall order and one that is inherently loaded for failure.

Express yourself
- Do communicate. Poor communication is the most widespread cause of stress in relationships. How well you communicate is a barometer of the quality of the relationships you have – good communicators are usually blessed with sunny weather!

If both parties work hard at expressing themselves, then a relationship has a chance to grow and blossom. So, it is important that you tell those to whom you are close your expectations, hopes, and aspirations – for your own good and for the good of the relationship.

Do you let people get close to you? Do your friends, family or even your partner know what you really feel? Or do you hide and bury your feeling for fear of rejection or misunderstanding? If you do not express your innermost feelings, resentment can build up which can sour a relationship. Clear and honest communication is the key to keeping stress at bay. Remember that a shared 'weakness' usually provides a stronger bond than a shared 'strength'.

Learn to listen
- How often have you begun a conversation with a friend only to find yourself speaking into thin air? There are few things more infuriating than discovering that not one word you have said has been taken in. But are you guilty of this crime, too?

Stress can be avoided in a relationship by listening carefully to what the other person has to say. Often, our instinct is to try to apportion blame for why things have gone wrong, to assume too much, or even to be too preoccupied with our own feelings.

When you listen carefully to what is being said, there is always something new to hear. And do not interrupt – let the other person have his or her say.

Be informed
- Do get more information. To prevent stressful situations building up at home or work, always try to get

more information. If, for example, your partner is constantly quizzing you about where you and your friends go after work or about the clothes you buy with your money, rather than having a stand up shouting match about how you hate his or her possessive attitude, try to get more information without sounding accusatory. Use a calm assertive manner and say, 'When you keep checking up on me I feel unhappy about having to answer everything in detail. It makes me think you don't trust me. What are you worried about?' *(Also see Chapter Ten: Assert Yourself.)*

• Do give more information. Stress can build up in a **Give feedback** relationship if you do not provide feedback. If your partner is always making jokes at your expense, especially in front of friends, then it is important to tell him or her that you do not appreciate being the butt of the humour.

Open communication can stop misunderstandings from developing. It also helps to keep a relationship in a healthy state and prevents long-term stress situations from building up.

• Do not take people for granted. In any relationship it **Appreciate others** can be very easy to forget what another's friendship or love means to us. It is equally too easy to criticize and focus on a person's faults.

If you are aware that you do this, try to stop. Show appreciation and tolerance and do not be reluctant to give praise when it is due. You can avoid relationship stress by respecting others and acknowledging their contribution.

• Do keep your word. Sometimes people use a variety **Do what you say** of excuses for not keeping their word – 'I've got to work late' must be one of the most overused. As far as possible, do not make promises unless you can keep them.

Intimate relationships In a relationship with your spouse or partner, the dos and don'ts listed above apply, but you also need to consider a few more methods for keeping the relationship stress-free.

Quality time The more quality time – time together doing positive things – you spend with your partner, the closer you become. An intimate relationship, like a plant, needs nurturing. Book time in your diary to spend quality time together or make a date to go out.

Personal space For a relationship to thrive, you also need personal space and time. Close intimate relationships often work best when you respect the other person's need for space – space in which they can pursue a hobby or an interest that is special to them. Ironically, the quality of time spent together often depends on the quality of time spent apart.

Is this what you both want? This brings us back to communication. Taking time to revise and review the past together – as well as planning ahead so that both of your needs and aspirations are met – can help a relationship to grow stronger.

Perhaps one of you wants children and the other does not; or one of you wants to move house and other cannot stand the idea. These are potentially stressful situations that can be avoided by calm discussion in which the needs of both of you are taken into account.

Joint responsibility A relationship is a two-way process and its success depends on both partners taking responsibility for it. If your relationship is not going well, the only way to improve it is for each of you to take responsibility for the way you feel. Only then will you be able to steer your relationship towards healthy positive change.

Steps towards a healthy relationship Write down ten ways in which you think you could improve your relationships, both at home and at work. For example, you could take your partner away for a weekend or you may decide to discuss your workload with your boss instead of worrying about it.

Chapter Ten

Assert Yourself

Some people can speak their minds. They have no problem telling the boss that they cannot work late or letting somebody know what they think of them. They invariably do so with just the right turn of phrase so that the person on the receiving end is not offended. Sometimes, they are even respected for their honesty!

Then there is another group of people who seem to go through life lost for words, unable to say what is on their minds, or able to stand up for themselves over the smallest matter. If you belong to this group, you will know only too well that immensely stressful situations occur when you are unable to express your needs effectively. When this happens, feelings of losing control typically take over.

To get the balance right is a simple matter of learning how to assert yourself. When you confront a person or situation in an assertive manner, it helps you to stay calm and enables you to create a win-win position. In this chapter, we will be looking at how communication can help you stay in control of stressful events.

Communication explained

There are three different styles of communication – passive, aggressive and assertive. You probably have an inkling as to which category you slot into but it is worth clarifying each style, nevertheless.

Passive communication

You may recognize this type of behaviour in people who always try to please others and avoid conflict at all costs. Their characteristics include a meek, compliant and long-suffering attitude. The passive communicator uses phrases like, 'If you wouldn't mind,' 'Sorry to bother you,' and 'Is that all right?' He or she will often avoid eye contact, may be softly spoken, and have a self-pitying attitude.

This kind of behaviour reflects the fact that passive communicators have withdrawn into themselves to avoid any potential confrontation, so that the stress of

71

the moment seems instantly relieved. Passive people invite others to take advantage of them and, while they may feel resentful and angry about the situation, they will tend to suffer in silence.

Aggressive communication

Aggressive people tend to bully others and step on their rights in order to protect their own. They are character-ized as domineering or forceful. Phrases like 'You'd bet-ter ...,' 'You're a typical ...,' or 'Stupid ...' are a common part of their speech.

Body language can also indicate aggressive com-municators: clenched fists, finger pointing, leaning forward and glaring, and talking loudly are a just a few characteristic signs. This kind of behaviour is often an abuse of power.

Assertive communication

Assertive communicators are clear, direct and honest. They are often described as thoughtful, optimistic, ratio-nal and decisive. They use phrases like 'I want ...,' 'I feel ...,' 'Let's do ....,' and 'What do you think?' Their body language reflects their self-confidence – they stand straight and steady, and speak clearly with assurance.

Communicating in a passive or aggressive way may appear to relieve or deflect stress instantly but either can become a burden in the long-term. Learning to communicate assertively may take time but, once mas-tered, you will find that your new manner can relieve stress just as instantly as your old method of communi-cation – with none of the long-term effects. You will also find that assertive behaviour boosts your self-con-fidence, earns you respect, and increases your odds of winning.

How do you communicate?

Perhaps you are not entirely sure of how you come across to others – you may think you are being assertive when in fact you are being aggressive. It is easy to fool yourself into thinking favourably about yourself. Read the statements below and compare them with how you would respond to the request that you work late to finish a report, knowing that you had already agreed to meet a friend.

- 'OK, I'll ring my friend and cancel my arrangements.'
- 'No, my contract says I finish at five, so you will have to get someone else to do it. I'm leaving now.'
- 'I understand the report has to be done urgently but I can't do it tonight. I'll come in early tomorrow to finish it.'

The first reply is passive, the second aggressive and the third assertive. If you would have answered with a passive or aggressive response, then your style of communication could be contributing to some of the stress that you are experiencing in your life. Now is the time to start learning how to assert yourself.

Outlined below are three steps you can use to help you become more assertive in your dealings with others. Start by using the steps in less important situations. As you become more skilful in applying them, your confidence levels will soar and your stress plummet. If you feel you would like more, assertiveness training is available at evening classes and, of course, group training has the added advantage of allowing you to practise techniques in role play.

Three steps to becoming an assertive communicator

Learning to say 'No' to others when appropriate, and 'Yes' to yourself, are good stress-reducing habits to get into. They will stop you trying to be all things to all people and will free up your personal time so that you can do the things that you really want to do.

1. Learn to say 'No'

Saying 'Yes' when it would be best to say 'No' increases the likelihood that you will be asked to do the same thing again. And, in time, an unbalanced relationship with the asker of the questions will develop. The snag is that saying 'No' in an assertive way requires you to believe in yourself and what you are saying. In addition, you must learn to phrase your sentences in a polite but nevertheless firm way. Here is an example of an assertive response – the sort of thing you need to practise saying.

Imagine that a very good friend asks you to go on

holiday to an exotic location. It sounds fantastic but you know that you will not enjoy doing the same things together and that, most importantly, you will ultimately be wasting time and money.

You know that you have to refuse and that, to be convincing, you have to do so assertively: 'Thank you for asking me, but I don't think that you and I would enjoy the same type of holiday. I think you should ask someone else.' There are, however, some people who do not seem able to take 'No' for an answer and you may need use a 'broken record technique' and calmly repeat yourself until the questions are no longer asked.

2. Mastering the broken record technique

When you want something done about a situation and you know you are within your rights but you are repeatedly told that it is not possible, the time is right for you to use the broken record technique. You might use the technique if, for example, the heel falls off a pair of shoes that are only a month old you are quite within your rights to ask for a new pair.

Calmly ask for what you want and keep repeating the request until your persistence pays off. The broken record technique does not always guarantee success but it does increase your odds and decrease your stress.

The technique can be applied in almost any situation. For example, when people try to fob you off with poor service. A good case in point was when I left my car with the garage for a check-up. I was promised that it would be ready for collection at 5.30 that evening. I arrived on time to pick it up, only to be told that it would not be ready until the next morning. I was infuriated, especially as the mechanics were still working. I took a deep breath and calmly but firmly said, 'I have to have the car this evening and, as the mechanics are still working, I am happy to wait for it to be done.' I kept on repeating the statement and eventually an agreement was reached. I drove home in my car an hour later!

3. The 'DESC' technique

This is another useful technique for tackling potentially stressful situations and enabling you to become more adept in expressing yourself assertively. DESC stands for Describe, Express, Specify and Consequences, and the technique is most effective when combined with 'I' statements that avoid blaming others. Use of the DESC formula is especially practical in situations such as when a friend keeps cancelling your tennis game at the last minute for no good reason.

- Describe. Be specific and focus on the problem. State the facts without being emotional. 'When you keep cancelling our tennis game at the last minute...
- Express. Let the other person feel how important the issue is to you. Use 'I' messages so it is clear that you are not blaming him or her. '...I feel let down and upset.'
- Specify. Be specific and firm in one or two sentences. State your wants or preferences, not commands. 'I would like you to let me know well in advance if you are going to cancel the game.'
- Consequences. Clarify the positive or negative consequences of your request. 'If you don't let me know in advance I think we should stop playing together,' or, 'If you do let me know in advance, it gives me time to find another partner.'

To help you to recognize in which areas of your life you need to make an effort to be more assertive and, consequently, the areas in your life that are stressful, it can be useful to make a list. Write down ten situations where you would like to be more assertive. Now list them in order of difficulty, the most difficult being the one that is also the most stressful. Writing down a list of situations in which you would like to be more assertive serves two purposes. First, it highlights situations that you might otherwise prefer to keep hidden. Secondly, once you have identified a situation on paper, you are more likely to consider it seriously and take action.

Assertive behaviour hierarchy

Your list may include tackling your boss for a salary increase or asking your partner to clean the bath after he or she has finished. If you rate asking for a salary increase as the most difficult and most stressful thing

75

to do, this would be number one on your list. While the bath cleaning question is a tough one, you may give it a stress rating of just five. Once you have compiled the list, use the three techniques we have already discussed in the chapter to help you get the results you require.

Assertive behaviour hierarchy

Situations in which to be more assertive

1. Questioning Jack's insane desire to shoot traffic lights.
2. Correcting Arthur (my boss) over (his) mistakes.
3. Saying 'No' to James (colleague) when he asks me to do some photocopying that 'won't take a minute'.
4. Questioning the plumber next time he comes about his exorbitant call-out fee.
5. Telling Ron (my secretary) to be more punctual in the mornings.
6. Asking questions at parent-teacher meetings.
7. Telling queue bargers at the bus stop where to get off.
8. Asking for identification when the meter reader comes.
9. Telling children not to drop litter in the park.
10. Washing up – why is it always me?

Chapter Eleven

Instant Ways to Manage Your Time

Does time seem to slip through your fingers? Do days, weeks and months disappear without you accomplishing much of anything, even though you were constantly busy? How you manage your time can have either a positive or negative effect on your stress levels and overall wellbeing.

Time can be your enemy or your friend – it all depends on how you use it. If you are the kind of person who tries to cram too much into a short space of time and is always in a hurry, or one who feels life is a never ending fight against the clock, you will know just how stressful it can be if you do not manage your time efficiently.

It is an obvious point, but time spent is gone forever. Unfortunately, the benefits of time travel are not available to us yet, so we cannot go back and finish the things we did not get done yesterday. Whether we like it or not, we are stuck with twenty-four hours a day. So rather than waste time, learn to make better use of it.

The following techniques will help you to use your time more effectively and avoid the worry of not having enough time to do what you want.

Set goals

One of the most important ways to manage your time successfully is to set goals – daily, weekly, monthly, annually and long-term. Without a clear picture of where you want to go, it is next to impossible to plan your life. Achieving your goals, however, will only ever be successful if you are realistic about your aims and your timescale – set them too high and it can add extra pressure to your life.

Setting yourself unrealistic goals is like turning on an auto-pilot button marked 'failure'. For example, deciding to learn a new language when you work or a have a family to take care of is a big commitment. Opting for a part-time course which can be handled in short sessions will take longer to complete than a crash course, but there is less chance of you becoming overwhelmed by the workload and running the risk of never finishing it.

Get yourself a piece of paper and a pen, and write down your key goals for the next year. They can be big or small and your list should include all those things that you have been meaning to do but have not had time for.

Now read over your list. The tasks probably look impossible. But they are not, provided you are realistic about your ambitions. Working from your list, decide what you can feasibly achieve this month. Then make a second list of practical small steps that will help you to get closer to your goals. If you want to learn golf, this month's task could be to find three golf clubs in your area. It may not seem a lot, but it is that all important step in the right direction.

Above all, the stages on your list must be achievable, which means that they must fit in with other parts of your life. If they do not, you run the danger of trying to do too much and, hey presto, you become stressed out.

If you find it difficult to to get your goals into perspective, break down each one into small, manageable chunks and then take each chuck one a step at a time. Here are three steps you can use to help you achieve what you want within a realistic timescale.

Step one: create a 'to do' list

Once you have identified your goals, the next step is to order them using 'A', 'B' and 'C' lists. The 'A' list is for activities which must get done – for example, buying a present for your son's birthday tomorrow. The 'B' list is for those activities you would like do to, and need to be done, but it will not be the end of the world if they are left until tomorrow, such as phoning a friend. The 'C' list is for those activities you would like to get done once you have completed your 'A' and 'B' lists, such as going shopping for clothes.

Step two: make a schedule

When you have ordered your goals, schedule them into your day. In this way they will not be shunted to the back of your brain where they could be forgotten.

This may sound odd, but it is just as important as your lists of things to do. Think about it – how much time do you waste on things that you would rather not do? Well, now is your chance to cut them out of your life.

Step three: create a 'not to do' list

Making a list of things that you do not want to do will help you to focus on and eliminate some of the things in your life that rob you of precious time. You could also draw up a list of all the time-wasting activities that you want to change, such as watching most uninteresting television programmes or chatting to somebody at work who is always negative.

As far as possible, cut out the unproductive elements of your life and start reducing those time-wasters to one or two a day until you have learnt to use your time more productively.

Listed below are a series of hints and tips that will enable you to manage your time more efficiently. Some may appear obvious but it is amazing how often they are ignored, usually by those who say that they have no time for anything.

Dos and don'ts of time management

'Don't put off until tomorrow what can be done today' is an old saying but it has more than a gram of common sense about it. Avoid postponing unpleasant activities – put them at the top of your list and get them out of the way. An additional bonus of good time management is that the more you respect your time, the more others will respect it too.

Avoid procrastination

Are you alert in the morning but fit to drop by four in the afternoon, or are you sluggish until noon and bright by the evening? We all have our own internal biorhythm which marches along to its own personal beat. Get to know when you operate at your best and use that time to complete important tasks.

Know your time zones

'How?' I hear you scream. It is simple – do not answer the telephone if you do not want to be disturbed and do not accept callers between certain times. If that is impossible, ask your secretary, a colleague or family

Avoid interruptions

member to take messages. Better still, invest in an answering machine and call back later. Let friends or colleagues know when you are not available – this will stop them dropping by for a chat and a cup of coffee.

Learn to say 'No' Use assertiveness techniques to avoid unrealistic demands *(see Chapter Ten: Assert Yourself)*.

Do one thing at a time Trying to do too many things at once is very stressful and can lead to mistakes and accidents. Discipline yourself to concentrate on the task in hand.

Take a break Use a relaxation technique in between each task to re-energize yourself *(see Chapter Twelve: Relaxation Techniques)*.

Delegate You do not have to be a super-being to stay in control. Learn how to delegate any jobs that can be handled by others – that way you stay in control of your work and not vice versa.

Spend less time in stressful situations If you know that certain situations are stressful, then schedule less time in these settings. If visiting your in-laws always ends in arguments, arrange to spend a couple of hours with them rather than a whole day. Also, avoid being a martyr – as far as possible steer clear of people who are always angry, miserable, or just plain annoying.

Invest some time Put aside some time to plan and get organized. Once this is done, you will find that you can do everything you want to do, and more, with less stress.

Chapter Twelve

Relaxation Techniques

How often do you relax? I mean really relax – not just a snatched cup of coffee and five minutes in front of the television but a complete unwind. Sadly, few of us do it often enough.

Relaxation is vital to health and wellbeing – everyone needs to recuperate both during and at the end of a busy day. If you do not give yourself time to relax, you could develop some of the stress symptoms we discussed in Part One. Relaxation helps you to focus on the present or, as Zen Buddhists believe, you become present in the moment and unconcerned about the past or the future.

It is only comparatively recently that the benefits of relaxation have been acknowledged by doctors and psychologists. Relaxation is now recognized as an important aid to creativity – often, it is when we relax that solutions to problems and good ideas seem to pop into our heads as if by magic. All too frequently, however, many of us turn to inappropriate aids to help us relax – tobacco, anti-depressants and copious amounts of alcohol are perennial favourites. While resorting to drugs may seem to provide a short-term answer, they are no more than a quick fix and can have very serious detrimental effects on health in the long-term.

In this chapter there is a questionnaire which will enable you to discover just how well – or badly – you relax at the moment. Following this, there is an introduction to the relaxation CD and information on a variety of relaxation techniques. When you get to the exercises, the key to success is to try not to try. You cannot force yourself to relax, so do not worry about how well you think you are doing.

Complete the questionnaire which is designed to give you an idea of how well you relax. Tick one of the boxes opposite each question and then tally up your

How well do you relax?

score. Give yourself 3 points for each Always box you tick, 2 points for each Sometimes box, and 1 point for each Seldom box. If your total number of points lies between 15 and 18, you have a good ability to relax; if you score between 11 and 14, you have an average ability to relax; and if you score between 6 and 10 you have a low ability.

Tick one of the boxes opposite each question that you think most applies to you.

How well do you relax?

	Always	Sometimes	Seldom
Are you able to concentrate on one problem at a time?			
Do you plan your day to include relaxing activities, e.g. a walk, listening to music, meeting friends?			
Are you able to shut out your worries when you go to bed?			
Do you adjust your body position when you are working to prevent tension building up?			
Do you regularly check yourself for tension habits, e.g. hunched shoulders, clenched fists?			
Do you plan your life to include changes of people, surroundings, activities?			

Inner calm with your relaxation CD The CD included in this kit provides you with an easy way to begin experiencing the benefits of deep relaxation. By setting aside just twenty minutes a day to listen to the CD, you can give yourself peace of mind during which you can let go of tension, clear away any negative thoughts, and re-energize yourself. At the same time, you can reprogramme your mind with positive thoughts and images.

The beneficial effects of using the CD are cumulative. During the first listening, you may find it difficult to let go and relax as you concentrate on following the instructions. But each time you play it, you will find it easier. Some people even fall asleep. If this happens, do not worry – the CD is programmed to wake you up at the end. You may think that all this sounds a bit like a mild form of hypnosis. In which case, you would, in fact, be right – this gentle type of hypnosis is both soothing and comforting. Above all, it is relaxing and completely safe.

Before you start listening, you may find it useful to use a Stressdot® to check out your tension levels. Remember, black or red are signs of stress; green and blue show that you are relaxed. When you have listened to the CD, check the dot again to see how the colour has changed.

How to use your CD

- Find a comfortable, quiet place to sit or lie down. Switch off the telephone (or take it off the hook) and make sure that you will not be disturbed. Close your eyes and follow the instructions on the CD. No real effort is required as the music and my voice will take you into deep relaxation.
- To begin with, just play Track 1 every day for approximately two weeks. When you feel that you can relax quite easily while listening to Track 1, move on to Track 2. Track 2 contains more music and fewer instructions. In time, you may find it particularly useful to play Track 2 at bedtime as it will help you sleep.
- As you become more relaxed in your daily life, play whichever track you prefer three or four times a week, or as often as you need. Gradually, you will find that you have more energy – your stress-induced symptoms will start to disappear, your concentration will improve, and you will feel a greater sense of happiness and wellbeing. You will also be less prone to illness.
- You can use the CD at any time – day or night. It is neither harmful nor addictive in any way at all. Most people choose a time that fits easily into their routine – after work, for example, so that they are relaxed and refreshed to enjoy the evening.

83

Experiment by listening to the CD at different times of the day until you find the time that best suits your needs. There is just one word of warning: **never play the CD when you are driving a car or using machinery.**

Breathe stress away

The quick-acting relaxation techniques outlined below can be used as 'first aid' whenever it is necessary to deal with a stressful situation. As you have probably already realized, breathing tends to hasten when you are stressed. Luckily, the reverse is also true – if you can control your breathing to a normal rate, the effects of the stress are reduced. Amazing but true!

Say, for example, you feel harassed. You are stuck in a long queue with only a few minutes to spare before you should be at work. You have a long hectic day ahead. What happens to your body? Your breathing becomes fast, shallow and irregular. This physical reaction is your body's way of coping with the short bursts of energy you might need to fight or take flight.

Over the long-term, this kind of breathing can have a detrimental effect on your mind and body. But, by consciously changing your breathing patterns, you can keep cool and clear-headed, even in the most stressful situations. Practise the breathing exercises listed below – anywhere, any place – on a regular basis to stress-proof yourself and to prevent stress symptoms from developing.

Six point plan for calmer breathing

1. Sit back in a comfortable chair (if this is not possible, shrug your shoulders, and relax your chest as best you can).
2. Concentrate on breathing slowly and deeply. Try to sustain a rhythm and avoid panting.
3. As you breathe in, feel your abdomen rise. Gently count one, two, three.
4. Breathe out and slowly let your abdomen fall back to normal. As you do so, count one, two, three.
5. With your lungs empty, pause for a moment for a count of three.
6. Repeat steps 3 to 5 about ten times. When you do this,

you will discover that your mind calms itself down and that your immediate feelings of stress diminish.

Guided imagery for relaxation

Relaxation is nature's own tranquillizer – the production of adrenaline is cut, muscles soften, and the brain switches into soft-peddle mode. One of the easiest ways to restore order to chaos is to conjure up peaceful and relaxing images. If you think that this sounds like an impossible task, or one that seems unlikely to have any effect, you are probably the sort of person who will gain the most from the exercise given below! Regardless of whether you are working in an office where the telephones never stop ringing or at home looking after screaming children, it is possible to take a 'time out'. Believe it or not, by practising the 'guided imagery' technique you can calm your mind in just a few minutes.

Remember, however, that you cannot force yourself to relax. When practising guided imagery, your mind may be racing with the million·and one things you have to do. Do not try to force images into your mind. Instead just allow them to form and be patient – to start with, keep each session short.

Quiet-place relaxation

- Close your eyes and think back to a place where you have been calm and peaceful. Visualize the surroundings – see the colours, hear the sounds. Allow these images to take you deeper into relaxation.
- Notice how relaxed you feel in this quiet place.
- Allow yourself to feel safe and secure in your own relaxation. Retreat and stay there for as long as you wish.
- When you are ready, open your eyes. Take a few deep breaths and savour that feeling of calmness.

This quiet-place technique can by used instead of a coffee break to recharge your energy levels to give immediate stress relief.

Seven instant relaxation techniques

The following techniques can be used to help you deal with stress in situations where you need to be cool and calm on the spot – for example, when giving

85

a presentation or attending an important interview. Quick relaxers can also recharge your resources when you are feeling tired and under pressure – stroking a passive pet can reduce tension in no time, as anyone who owns a cat will know.

It is important to know that the beneficial effects of these techniques is only temporary. For long lasting results, you should practise them in conjunction with the techniques covered earlier in the chapter.

Shrug your shoulders

Stress caused by anxiety, frustration or worry, most often affects the body in the shoulders and neck. Muscles tense up and headaches invariably follow. This exercise can promote relaxation, not just in the neck, but throughout the body.

- Simply, shrug your shoulders – once quite quickly, then again slowly. Repeat the exercise as often as you need to loosen muscles and relieve their tautness.

Stretch

Like the shoulder shrug, a good stretch can release tension in your whole body, possibly more so. If you have a tendency to hunch your shoulders, a healthy stretch is often what you need to ease muscles.

- Stand up straight and raise your hands above your head. Hold your breath as your stretch your hands towards the ceiling. As you breathe out, let go of the tension and allow yourself to flop down like a rag doll. You should only need to do this once.

Cue phrase

Make up a positive phrase that is easy to remember, such as, 'I feel calm and relaxed' or, 'I can do it.' Use this phrase as your personal 'coping motto'.

- In your moment of crisis, close your eyes and take a few deep breaths. As you breathe in, repeat your chosen phrase and, as you breathe out, say the words again. Repetition of the phrase will boost your confidence and relieve stress – it is a technique often used by top track athletes before major events.

Listen to music

It is a well known fact that music can help people to relax and also change mood. What kind of music you listen to is relevant to the way you are feeling.

- For total relaxation, choose sounds of the sea or bird songs. Alternatively, you might like to listen to some soothing classical music or bebop jazz.
- For energy, opt for upbeat music, be it pop, inspiring classical music or rock-'n'-roll.

One year from now

If you are in a situation where you know you have made a mistake, you have said something stupid, or made a fool of yourself, it can help to release tension by thinking about what the consequences of your action will mean in the future.

- Ask yourself, 'Will all this matter one year from now?' It is a simple statement but an effective one. You will be surprised at how quickly your problem, and how to deal with it, falls into perspective.

Foot massage

Your poor feet carry a burden day in, day out. Is it any wonder that they occasionally feel the strain? Tender feet invariably carry an equally tender body and gentle massaging can help to relieve tension right the way up, through your spine, to your skull.

- Take off your shoes and socks and place a small, firm ball – a squash ball is ideal – beneath your right foot. Roll it gently around in small circles, making sure you cover the whole of your sole. Do this for about three minutes, closing your eyes as you enjoy the massage. Repeat the massage on your left foot to balance up the treatment.

Take time out

This is a quick and easy way to clear your head in the midst of chaos. Simply leave the crisis environment – your office, the house, whatever – and take five minutes to walk around. This will create a physical and mental distance between you and your stress situation. You can then return refreshed and ready for action.

Chapter Thirteen

See the Funny Side

How often have you referred to someone who makes you laugh as being 'a real tonic'? It is a good phrase because laughter can be just that, a tonic. In Britain and America the development of laughter clinics to treat illnesses like depression highlights the fact that laughing is now being taken seriously.

The man who has done more than most to show that laughter can have a healing influence is the American, Norman Cousins. In his compelling book, *Anatomy of an Illness* (W.W. Norton & Company, Inc. 1979), Cousins relates how he recovered from a potentially fatal illness by collecting all the humorous material he could find – books, films, recordings and so on – and literally laughed himself back to health.

It is a truism to say that one of the healthiest things you can do when feeling stressed is to substitute a negative thought with a humorous one. I am not talking about wry or cynical humour but the kind of humour that makes you laugh in spite of yourself. If you stop to think about it, it is difficult, if not impossible, to remain tense and to laugh at the same time – a good side-splitting laugh, the kind that makes you double over or reduces you to tears is one of nature's own stress-breakers and instant refreshers.

Learn to laugh at yourself You only have to watch a situation comedy on television to realize that it is usually the unexpected or exaggerated suggestions that make you laugh. One tactic that comedians use to do this is to make fun of themselves, to send up their faults and troubles. While you may not want millions of strangers laughing at your problems, if you can make yourself laugh about your problems, your stress will instantaneously melt away. Looking for the funny side of your situation can also help to remind you that most of your problems are not unique and that you are by no means alone in experiencing them.

Internal jogging

Laughter can also have a positive physiological effect on your body; it has, in fact, been described as 'internal jogging'. A good laugh speeds up your breathing, increases your heart rate and body temperature, and triggers the release of natural pain-killing chemicals. As you wait for the punch line of a joke, your muscles tense in anticipation and when you burst out laughing, they contract. This process sets up a relaxation response which can last up to forty-five minutes as your body recovers from the excitement.

Laughing with others

How many times do you laugh during the day? If you are not laughing that often, think about changing the company you keep; find people who make you laugh and try to spend more time with them. If you are blessed with a good sense of humour, remember to hold on to it in stressful times. It may seem inappropriate to laugh or crack a joke in the middle of a crisis but it could be just the outlet you need.

If you want to feel more relaxed, start introducing humour slowly into situations where you do not have much to lose – with friends or family.

Small doses at first

To capitalize on the tension-releasing effects of humour, knowing when to use it is vital. Cracking jokes at the wrong moment can be annoying for those around you; adding humour slowly and with moderation, however, can have a great many benefits. Try the following exercises to begin the process.

- Imagine a person who is annoying you as a cartoon caricature that always makes you laugh.
- Imagine someone in authority in a compromising position, for example, sitting in their underwear.
- Think of someone who makes you laugh and see that person on a regular basis.
- Plan to watch funny movies or comedy shows as often as you can.
- When you feel low, make a concerted effort to smile. You will find that this has an uplifting effect on you and everyone around you.

Chapter Fourteen

Travel Stress

The problem with travel is that there are so many things which can go wrong that are out of our control. We all know what it is like to sit in a traffic jam because a set of traffic lights has broken down. And who has not been held up at an airport, waiting for a plane that has been held up by fog, a storm or a strike? Even the simplest journey can be blighted by roadworks and, especially for those of us who live in towns and cities, commuting or taking the children to school can become a major source of stress. In fact, for many of us, travel is just another word for stress.

In Chapter Two, we looked at how evolution has equipped the human body to respond to a crisis. All the stress mechanisms fire up at once and our aggression rises ready for fight or flight. If you sit in a traffic jam with little hope of it clearing quickly, frustration can bubble over causing you to fight because you cannot run away. Some people who are normally polite and well-mannered turn into vengeful maniacs when they are sandwiched in a bumper-to-bumper crawl. They take it out on their cars by banging the steering wheel or by shouting obscenities at other drivers.

All this fury will, however, have little effect on your situation – it certainly will not get the traffic moving any quicker. All that happens is that you arrive at your destination late, angry and frustrated. But travelling does not need to be like this.

Be a travel survivor The best way to deal with travel stress, is to recognize that it can be stressful and to prepare yourself before you start a journey. A few simple measures can turn travelling into an opportunity rather than a crisis – then, the time you spend travelling will have fewer bad effects and more beneficial ones. The following tips apply whether you are using public transport or are travelling in the comfort of your car.

Be realistic

It almost goes without saying, but leave for your destination in plenty of time. Because most of us hate the hassle of travelling, we put off leaving until the latest possible moment. This is where most travellers' troubles begin, so, do not cut it too finely.

The closer you are to your destination the easier it is to do this. You may theoretically live just twenty minutes from the airport but you only have to encounter two red lights, an old person crossing the road, and a broken-down car, for your journey to catch a plane to turn into a heart-stopping dash if you leave with exactly twenty minutes in hand. Is that extra five minutes in bed really worth it?

Travelling to a new place

When you are setting off for somewhere new, planning is essential. Prepare yourself by studying maps and routes. Ask around, someone at work or a friend may have made the same journey and may be able to give you tips on short-cuts or the roads to avoid. There are even several service companies which can plan your route for you.

Plan for a hold up

You never know when you are going to hit a trouble spot or a major delay, so be prepared for the worst. Take with you on your journey a good book, a personal stereo, or even work from the office – anything that will help to pass the time. While you may not be able to control what is going on outside, you can run your own show and take control of the situation if you are well prepared.

Practise relaxation exercises

Some of the instant relaxation techniques described in Chapter Twelve will give you just the quick fix you need to help you stay calm. Do not, however, play the relaxation CD.

At regular intervals roll your shoulders and stretch your legs. Stops at traffic lights can be a signal to loosen up and adjust your body position.

Enjoy the time

If you are sitting in your car in the middle of a traffic snarl up, avoid listening on the radio to the news of the disaster that has brought your journey to a stop.

Replaying it over and over again will only serve to wind you up. Instead, listen to a different radio station or play one of your favourite tapes or CDs.

Day dreaming Travelling is often a good time to plan other activities – your holiday, new business strategies, or even menus for the week. Solutions for all sorts of problems can be wrestled with while you are forced to sit still. If you can, keep a portable cassette recorder in your car and use it as a note book – empty your thoughts on to it or dictate letters.

Alternatively, while away the minutes by watching and observing other people as they hustle their way to work or browse in shop windows. Watching other people is a truly fascinating pastime!

Study while you are stationary When your car is forced to a standstill, your brain does not have to do likewise. Use your travel time to learn a new skill or brush up on old ones. For example, you could learn a new language by listening to tapes or CDs.

Mobile telephone A 'hands-free' mobile telephone will enable you to make your calls while driving, or better still, while you are parked so that you can concentrate on the conversation. If necessary, you can also let people know that you are likely to be late – this in itself can ease your mind and reduce anxiety and stress.

Chapter Fifteen

Achieving a Balanced Lifestyle

The pressures and strains of modern life mean that we are constantly being pulled in different directions. Trying to please everyone is nigh on impossible and, as we have already discussed, stressful.

To some of us, life is a juggling act between work, rest and play, and getting the balance right – to please everybody – seems just about impossible. In this chapter, we will be looking at how you can achieve a balanced lifestyle by focusing on how you weigh up work, relationships, leisure, self-development and what I call 'Me' time. First, let us have a glimpse at how elements that go to make up a 'lifestyle' can be changed for the better.

Work

Is work taking over your life? Are the extra hours you spend in the office eating away at your leisure time or the time you might otherwise spend with your family? Everyone needs a challenge and work provides this for most people. However, too much challenge or involvement at work can turn a conscientious worker into a workaholic. If you know that your workload is too heavy, be assertive – talk it through with your boss and explain the problems.

Conversely, too little challenge – as happens when you are unemployed – can lead to boredom, stagnation and low self-esteem which is equally stressful. If this is the case, look for activities to fill up your life while applying for new jobs. Your local paper or library are good sources of information about local events – offer your services for free if necessary.

Relationships

It is important to get the balance right between the time you spend with acquaintances, family, and intimate friends. Be aware of letting one of these relationships take over too much of your time. If you feel too many demands are being made on you from any one quarter, this is when you need to be assertive and negotiate for compromise. There is no denying that the compromise may be difficult to achieve, and you always run the risk of upsetting someone, but in the long-run it is vital for your health and wellbeing.

> When Bill's company sports' day clashed with a regular visit to his partner's parents he was faced with a decision: he could either cancel the visit or miss the sports' day. Bill knew that the first course of action would run the risk of upsetting his partner and disappointing her parents, but he was also aware that his support at this high profile company event was important to his future. In the end Bill was able to reach a compromise by offering to visit the family the following weekend.

Leisure

For some of us, leisure time equates with luxury time – in other words, it rarely happens. This is a bad thing as leisure time is crucial to wellbeing.

Make the effort to plan your weekends and evenings as carefully as your workdays. This may prove to be a strain of a minor sort but you will find it revitalizing as well as stress-relieving in the long-term. You will also find that you get the more out of your leisure time as it will have been well planned in advance.

In addition, do not ignore the potential of hobbies, holidays and occasional breaks as these give you the opportunity to wind down negative feelings and wind up positive ones. One-off surprises apart, they usually need to be planned in advance and it is important to let other people who might be involved know what you have arranged – this will prevent tensions arising from misunderstandings.

Self-development

To stop stress building up in your life, it is important to be aware of your under-developed potential. By recognizing your weaknesses, and by doing something about them, you lessen the stress in your life. If, for example, you find it difficult to maintain relationships, seeing a therapist *(see Gaining Further Help, page*

108) could help you to overcome the problem. If you are overlooked for promotion at work, ask yourself why. Did the person who was promoted have more skills than you? If so, then this is the time to think about further training so that the next time promotion is offered you will be ready and equipped to meet the challenge.

'Me' time

If your life has become task-orientated, or if you find yourself spending too much time doing things for others, you need to take time out occasionally to indulge in 'Me' time – time spent by yourself, for yourself. 'Me' time can be crucial to many people's wellbeing and planning it in advance is often the only way to make sure that it materializes.

'Me' time should be your own exclusive time during which *you* do exactly what *you* want without feeling guilty. You could, perhaps, lie in bed late on a weekend morning listening to the radio. Or, you might treat yourself with a visit to an art exhibition. Make time for yourself and enjoy it!

How to achieve a healthy lifestyle

As part of a balanced lifestyle, you need to develop healthy practices to stress-proof yourself and give you energy and stamina to cope with the challenges of life. In this section of the chapter, we will be looking at some of the lifestyle changes you may need to make.

Get physical to control stress

Regular exercise is a vital element of stress control. This is because human bodies are basically designed for a primitive lifestyle – for hunting and for keeping warm – and not for today's sedentary ways where machines are used to replace muscle-power. In this day and age, bringing home food simply means driving the car to the supermarket and picking up the ready-hunted, and, in some cases, ready-cooked food; and keeping warm means switching on the central heating. Our bodies are no longer being asked to do what they are designed for, so we have to provide them with the physical exertion they need. If we do not provide our bodies with exercise, then our muscles and subsequently our minds, deteriorate.

How fitness beats stress

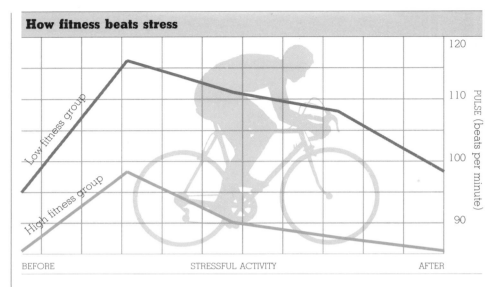

Low fitness group

High fitness group

120

110

100

90

PULSE (beats per minute)

BEFORE   STRESSFUL ACTIVITY   AFTER

The graph above shows how successfully fitness can combat stress, In a series of stress tests, a high fitness group recorded consistently lower pulse rates than unfit counterparts.

To remain fit and healthy, our bodies need to be kept active – exercise is, in effect, the closest we can usually come to in unleashing our fight or flight responses. Insufficient exercise may not affect us in the short-term but, without a physical outlet, stress can build up within our bodies and this can have serious consequences which can ultimately lead to illness. If you are one of those people who spends their days at a desk, arrives home exhausted, and sits down to a convenience meal in front of the television, it is time to take physical action!

The benefits of physical activity

Exercise reduces your adrenaline levels and triggers the release of endorphins – hormones which kill pain, lift spirits, and help your body to get back to normal after a stress attack.

After a difficult day, going to an exercise class or taking a dip in a swimming pool will help you thrash out pent-up aggression. Your head will feel clearer, your body re-energized, and you will generally feel calmer and more able to relax and enjoy your evening. Physical activity can help to make stress what should be: a brief helpful response to challenge rather than a permanent ball and chain.

Start gradually

Most people who try to get into shape after a period of inactivity are in too much a hurry. Unfortunately, there are no instant solutions to fitness and there is only a fine line that divides conditioning yourself and exhausting yourself.

Choose a sport or activity and start off slowly – if you have not run in years, you cannot expect to go out and run a five-minute mile straight away. Build up your stamina by exercising for increasingly longer lengths of time. In this way you will be motivated to keep to your programme. Trying to do too much, too soon, can be painful – it may even lead to injury and, as a result, you are more likely to give up.

Make it fun

Unfortunately, you cannot store the physical and psychological benefits of exercise in a cupboard and take them out when you need them. The only way you can reap the benefits is if you exercise regularly and, to do that, the sport or activity has to be fun, convenient and safe.

Choose an activity that you find genuinely enjoyable – if you hate water, avoid swimming. It sounds obvious, but if exercising becomes a chore, it is likely to do you more harm than good. And remember, exercising does not mean that you have to suffer for an hour among a mass of sweaty, heaving bodies in a trendy gym. Housework, gardening, mowing the lawn, walking the dog, and dancing all provide excellent physical exercise.

Convenience

Most of us will use the flimsiest of excuses not to exercise. And if it ever becomes remotely inconvenient, we will refuse to struggle to the pool or gym when we could be at home watching the television.

The trick of avoiding this scenario is to make your exercise sessions as convenient as possible. Plan to exercise when you know you will have time available. Leave your kit at work and go for a walk in your lunch break. Go to the swimming pool or gym on the way home from work rather than going home first – once you are home it is often hard to go out again.

Keep it safe If you have not exercised for a while, or have recently been ill, consult your doctor for a check-up before embarking on an exercise programme that will involve strenuous activity. While you are at your doctor's, why not use your appointment to discuss the best form of activity for you?

Always bear in the back of your mind that the goal of exercise is to train not strain. If you feel any pain, dizziness, or shortness of breath while exercising, stop immediately and pay your doctor a visit.

Set realistic goals Do not allow yourself to become too competitive if you are already stressed out – you will be simply piling one stress on top of another. Pushing yourself to beat your previous best, or to thrash your partner at squash, will add to the stress in your life, not reduce it. If you feel the need for more stress, fierce competition is fine. But if more stress is the last thing you need, avoid the temptation to goad yourself too hard – play to enjoy the activity rather than just to win.

Add variety If you get bored with one sport, switch to another – adding variety to your programme will help to keep you motivated. If you go to the gym, use a different piece of equipment each time you go. To ensure a balanced work-out, do something aerobic every other day.

Alternating activities in this way will also avoid stressing the same muscle groups on consecutive days. Try swimming one day and power walking the next for good all round fitness.

Walk to beat stress Brisk walking on a regular basis is a near-perfect way of exercising. Apart from a good pair of trainers, it costs nothing and can be done at any time, anywhere. Another bonus of walking is that it can be adjusted to suit your own level of fitness.

When walking for fitness, you need to stride fast enough so that you breathe deeply but are not short of breath. For best results walk for at least half an hour three or four times a week. The added advantage of walking over other activities is that everyone in the family can take part, making it an excellent form of family stress control.

To get into the habit of walking:

- Never drive less than one mile – make the decision to walk instead;
- Park your car further away from your destination than normal – this will make you walk a bit further;
- Get off the bus a stop earlier than usual and finish your journey on foot;
- Use stairs instead of taking a lift or escalator;
- Do not make bad weather an excuse not to walk – use an umbrella.

Eat to beat stress

A racing car cannot give its best on low quality fuel, and you cannot give your best living off a poor diet. If you drink coffee to keep going, eat more than you need for comfort, miss out on breakfast, rely on convenience foods or take-aways, you need to make changes to your eating habits.

When you are under stress, your body becomes more prone to digestive problems and your nervous system and adrenal glands work on overdrive, using up more nutrients than normal. Furthermore, when you are under pressure, healthy eating is likely to be low on your priority list, further depleting the body of essential vitamins and minerals.

It is possible, however, to counteract a good deal of the unwanted, negative effects of stress with a healthy balanced diet.

Eat little and often

Eat healthy regular meals and snacks throughout the day. This will help to keep your blood sugar levels steady and sustain your energy. Eating a good breakfast will keep you going throughout the morning and provide your body with vital mineral resources right from the beginning of the day.

Eat more fibre

A high-fibre diet will help to keep you healthy and may help to reduce cholesterol. Fibre is found in

99

wholefood bread and pasta, brown rice, vegetables and fruit, all of which can help with weight control. Increase the amount of fibre in your diet slowly so that it does not result in indigestion.

Avoid foods made with refined sugar Sugar is released during the stress response, but the temporary lift it gives you is quickly followed by chemically-induced weakness and fatigue. Taking in additional sugar in your diet compounds the problem, so substitute refined sugar for more complex carbohydrates such as bread, pasta and cereals.

Chew your food The first digestive step takes place in the mouth where chemicals in the saliva called enzymes begin to break down food. If you bolt down your food, you are skipping a vital stage in the digestive process; you are also more likely to eat more than you need. The result is that you end up with chronic indigestion – the last thing you want when stress is on the horizon.

Take time to eat Get into the habit of thinking that whatever needs to be done can wait for half an hour while you eat your meal. Stop what you are doing, move away from your desk or leave the office, and put some thought into what you eat.

Eating should be an enjoyable experience rather than just a fuel stop. Pause between mouthfuls and between courses. When you have finished your meal, give yourself time to digest your food before returning to your hectic schedule. If possible, eat with someone else as it is always more relaxing if you can have a conversation at meal times.

Relax when you eat Do not eat or drink when you are angry, upset or agitated. Practise a few relaxation exercises first or go for a walk. You will digest your food all the better for delaying your meal.

Eat early Try to eat your last meal at least three hours before going to bed. This gives your body time to digest the food properly and will help you to sleep better.

Watch the caffeine!

Coffee, tea and fizzy cola drinks all contain large amounts of caffeine. This gives the body a temporary lift – which is why we always want a cup of coffee or tea when we are tired – but it depletes the body of the vitamins and minerals it needs when it is under stress.

Do not lapse into the stress cycle of relying on a strong cup of coffee to soothe your frazzled nerves or to give you the energy to get you through the day. Too much caffeine is stress-inducing and can cause nervousness, insomnia, and irregular heartbeats. Opt for herbal teas, diluted fresh juices, or plenty of mineral water instead.

Avoiding food allergies

Caffeine and sugar are both common food allergens and can create stress symptoms – palpitations and nausea, for instance. But almost any food can cause problems in some people, so it can pay to be aware of how you may be reacting to food. Other common food allergens, like wheat and dairy products, can produce symptoms such as headaches, sleepiness, irritability, and joint pain, all of which look like stress and are definitely made worse by stress.

If you suspect you may have a food allergy, ask your doctor for an allergy test and then avoid the foods that are implicated. Unfortunately, some people find that they have a powerful craving for the foods that they are allergic to. Keep a food diary and rotate suspect foods so as to discover which are to be avoided.

Choose fresh food

Under stress your body needs more vitamins and minerals, so try to eat fresh foods. Home-cooked food is healthier than convenience food, take-aways and hamburgers, none of which provide the necessary nutrients your body needs to combat stress.

What to decrease and increase

Reduce your intake of red meat and salty foods, and also cut back on fat by using low-fat spreads and margarines. Grill, poach or steam your food in preference to frying. Fatty foods not only make you put on weight but they can also clog up your circulatory system and give you bad skin. Basically, an excessive intake of fat

101

strains the body's systems and hampers, rather than helps, when it comes to stress control.

Increase the amount of white meat, fish, fresh fruit, vegetables, wholemeal bread, wholewheat pasta, and brown rice in your diet. All these foods contain valuable nutrients and they do not cause you to put on weight if eaten in moderation. They are, in fact, a vital part of a healthy diet.

Stress busters In particularly stressful times you may wish to supplement your diet with extra vitamins if you know you are not eating properly. These can give you that much-needed vitamin boost but take care not to rely on supplements on a long-term basis – they are no substitute for a well-balanced diet.

Nutritionists now acknowledge the benefit of certain foods and vitamins for people under stress, in particular those containing vitamin C, vitamin B complex, zinc and magnesium. These provide the nutrients your adrenal glands need to make hormones, so it makes sense to increase these when you are under stress.

Good sources of vitamin C are broccoli, green peppers, cabbage, citrus fruits, and spinach. Vitamin B complex is found in wholegrain cereals, wholemeal bread, nuts, bananas and avocados. Zinc is found in greatest amounts in meat, dairy products, and eggs. And good sources of magnesium are nuts, wholegrain cereals and green vegetables.

If you think that your diet could be improved, make a commitment today to plan changes in the weak areas. List five ways you can do this and gradually introduce them into your routine.

The evils of drink A drink after work can help you to unwind and can provide you with the opportunity to talk to colleagues about your problems. But like any other drug, alcohol can be misused and is addictive.

Moderate drinking offers a short-term solution to stressful situations but overindulgence only serves to mask real problems, often setting up a vicious cycle which can be hard to break. How much is drink ruling your life? Consider the following questions and answer them honestly.

- Do you sometimes need a drink to face certain problems or situations?
- Has your work suffered because of your drinking?
- Have there been occasions when you felt unable to stop drinking?
- Do you hide how much you drink from family and friends?

What happens when you drink

If you answered yes to any one of the questions, you need to control your drinking before it starts controlling you. Most people make the mistake of thinking that alcohol is a stimulant because it helps them to relax and they become funny and talkative under its influence. But the reverse is in fact true – alcohol is a potent depressant.

Drinking when you are stressed can dull your body's ability to cope. It stimulates your gastric juices which increases the mayhem already going on in your overworked stomach. Alcohol also disrupts your mental performance and prevents you from working effectively.

How alcohol increases the stress in your life

The beneficial effects of alcohol are only ever short lived, which is fine if the stress is a temporary condition, too. However, long-term stress accompanied by long bouts of drinking will, in the end, only exacerbate your problems and this can have disastrous consequences on many areas of your life.

Work

It is easy to believe that drinking will ease the pressure at work and help you to solve your problems. In most instances quite the opposite is true and your ability to carry out your job may be adversely affected by alcohol.

Drinking may cause you to make costly errors at work or, even worse, cause accidents. It may also affect your timekeeping – if you start drinking heavily, you may suddenly realize that you are constantly late for appointments; you may even end up missing them completely because you are permanently nursing a hangover.

103

Home In the course of my work as a counsellor, I have found that alcohol plays a large part in many family arguments and marriage breakdowns. It is also the cause of a great deal of family violence. Drinking to excess will very often result in you neglecting yourself, your partner, and even your children.

Money Drink can also aggravate money problems. Alcohol is not cheap and you may spend more on it than you or your family can afford. This lack of money will trigger more arguments and increase your stress.

Social life When drink becomes the main activity in your social life, it can also affect your relationships. Friends will become tired of your constant drinking and may even lose sympathy for your problems. In the long run you may even lose them and their support and miss out on other positive activities.

Health Alcohol can have a detrimental affect on many organs of the body, not just the liver. It also depletes your stores of essential nutrients like vitamin A which is needed to maintain healthy skin, teeth and bones and is vital for healthy vision. Heavy drinkers increase the risk of a wide range of diseases compared to light or non-drinkers.

How to cut down on drink

- First identify the reasons behind your drinking behaviour. Do you drink to relax or to forget your worries? Or is it because you feel angry or because you are bored? Facing up to your feelings and writing down the things that are bothering you will help you to begin to take action in solving your problems.
- Make a contract with yourself or a friend to cut down by a certain amount and specify the time scale in which you will do it.
- Think of a reward you could give yourself when you achieve your goal – a weekend break or a new golf club, perhaps.
- Keep a drinking diary. Fill in each day with the times you drink heavily, in which places, and in whose company. Then work out how you can best avoid

these situations. Go to the cinema instead of the wine bar, or meet a friend who is teetotal.

- Plan how much you are going to drink before you go out and stick to it. You have to be strong, though, as your resolve will probably start weakening as soon as you have downed the first sip.

- Do not just sit down and drink when you go out. Start playing games such as darts, dominoes or pool.

- Always dilute your drink if you can. Top up spirits with plenty of mixer, take small sips and drink as slowly as possible.

- Finally, make a list of the ways in which you will cut down your drinking – this shows true commitment.

If you cannot stop

If you feel unable to cut down on your drinking by yourself and that you are physically dependant on alcohol, then you need specialist help. Make an appointment to see your doctor, a self-help group like Alcoholics Anonymous or a counsellor who specializes in alcohol addiction.

Smoking can seriously damage your health

Another activity many of us turn to when we are stressed is smoking. It gives us something to do with our hands and those long deep draws on a cigarette seem to have a steadying effect on our shaky nerves.

Here again, the short-term benefits are far out-weighed by the detrimental effects long-term. Smoking, like alcohol, depletes the body's store of vital nutrients and it can indisputably seriously damage your health. Like dodging traffic for a hobby or playing Russian roulette, smoking kills.

If you cannot quit by yourself

Wanting to give up smoking and actually succeeding are two different stories. To quit after several years of addiction requires a lot of willpower and determination. If you cannot give up on your own, alternative therapies like acupuncture and hypnosis can help. Alternatively, ask your family doctor for advice or look in your local library or health clinic for any stop smoking courses that may be running in your area – for example, many hospitals organize such courses.

Chapter Sixteen

The Dos and Don'ts of Stress Management

Dos This chapter sums up the key points in the book. It is a quick reference section – read through the lists whenever your life seems to be tilting off course so that you can get back on the right track quickly.

- Do take action. Anxious worrying will not solve your problems, so stop dithering around and do something positive.
- Do watch what you think and say. Negative words and phrases can hold you back and make you depressed. Think positive.
- Do watch your diet. Cut down on stimulants such as coffee, alcohol, sugar and junk food.
- Do be assertive. Say 'No' when you need to.
- Do have some comic relief. Avoid taking life too seriously; learn to appreciate the lighter side.
- Do manage your time efficiently. Planning ahead will give you more time to do what you want.
- Do pamper yourself. Take time out during the day just for you.
- Do express yourself. Try to build bridges rather than barriers; a quick chat with a friend may be all that you need.
- Do a stress 'clean out' at the end of every week. Think about what has caused you stress recently and reassess what you can do to eliminate the causes.
- Do seek professional help, if necessary. Recognize the danger signs and take action.

Don'ts
- Don't expect the worst to happen. What you believe often actually occurs.
- Don't overeat or use drugs, drink or tobacco as ways of running away from your problems.
- Don't allow others to take advantage of you. Be assertive and stand up for your rights.

- Don't put off dealing with stressful situations until they come to a head. Act now.
- Don't try to be a superperson. Your best is good enough.
- Don't bottle up your anger or frustration. This can lead to destructive behaviour. If necessary, and if possible, shout, scream or punch a pillow.
- Don't allow work to take over your life. Take time to plan a balanced lifestyle.
- Don't blame others as this is a waste of energy. Recognize that there is a problem and do something about it.
- Don't procrastinate and wait for stress to disappear by itself. If you do, it will only get worse.
- Don't be afraid to ask for help when you need it from family, friends or professionals.

A last word on stress

At the beginning of the book I explained that I wanted you to regard this kit as your personal tool box for handling stress. Take from it the bits you require, and ignore the bits for which you have no need. However, like all tool boxes, it may not have just the right spanner or wrench for your problem. If that is the case, refer to Gaining Further Help *(overleaf)*.

If this pack has helped you to see that your life does not have to go on the way it has, then it has succeeded. And I do hope that it has given you the determination to restore some balance to your life and to reduce your stress to a minimum so that you become happier, healthier and more fulfilled.

Gaining Further Help

In this section, you will find information on various therapies that can be used to ease stress as well as contact addresses, lists of recommended books, and sources of recordings that may be of help.

Therapies

'How do you go about finding someone you can trust?' This is a question most people ask when they first consider consulting an alternative therapist. One of the easiest ways is to consult your doctor; another is to take the recommendation of a friend. Alternatively, check out the notice board at your health centre or find an association which can refer you to a qualified, registered therapist in your area. Outlined below is essential information on different therapies, together with contact addresses for some of their organizations. As a general rule, it is best to contact an organization on the telephone first and then to send a stamped, self-addressed envelope for more information.

Acupuncture

Acupuncture is based on the belief that when your body is under stress your whole system becomes unbalanced. Needles are used to stimulate specific areas along energy channels. The aim of this treatment is to rebalance energy flow and so restore health.

- The Council for
  Acupuncture
  63 Jeddo Street
  London W12 9HQ
  Tel. 020 8350 0400

Alexander Technique

An educational technique to improve wellbeing. It teaches you to use your body more efficiently so as to avoid pain, strain and injury.

- Society for Teachers of the
  Alexander Technique
  20 London House
  266 Fulham Road
  London SW10 9EL
  Tel. 020 7284 3338

Aromatherapy

This therapy involves the use of essential plant oils to relieve stress, improve health, and prevent illness. The oils are massaged into the skin where they are absorbed by the blood stream.

- Aromatherapy Organization
  Council
  P. O. Box 19834
  London SE25 6WF
  Tel. 020 7251 7912

Bach Flower Therapy

This is a complete healing system used to treat emotional problems.The remedies, made from flowers, work to restore balance, a positive outlook and good health.

- Dr Edwards Bach Centre
  Mount Vernon
  Stotwell
  Wallingford
  Oxfordshire OX10 OPZ
  Tel. 01491 834678

Homeopathy

A treatment which works on the principle of 'like cures like' in which minute doses of animal, vegetable or mineral substances are administered. In large doses, these substances could cause symptoms similar to the illness.

- Society of Homeopaths
  4A Artisan Road
  Northampton NN1 4HU
  Tel. 01604 621400

Hypnotherapy

By allowing external distractions to fade, this therapy gives subjects the opportunity to focus on their problems and to change inappropriate behaviour, thoughts and feelings.

- Nation Council for
  Hypnotherapy Ltd
  P.O. Box 5779
  Burton on the Woulds
  Loughborough LE12 5ZF
  Tel. 01509 881477

Massage
This hands-on treatment seeks to maintain the balance of the body's systems. It can be used for relaxation, stress reduction or muscular problems.

- The British Massage
  Therapy Council
  17 Rymers Lane
  Oxford
  Oxon OX4 3JU
  Tel: 01865 774123

Osteopathy
A system of healing which works on the physical structure of the body. Practitioners use manipulation, massage and stretching techniques.

- The General Osteopathic
  Council
  Osteopathy House
  176 Tower Bridge Road
  London SE1 3LU
  Tel. 020 7357 6655

Psychotherapy
Psychotherapy is helpful in relieving deep-rooted emotional and behavioural problems. The therapy aims to bring conflicts back into the conscious mind so that they can be resolved.

- British Association of
  Psychotherapists
  37 Mapesbury Road
  London NW2 4HJ
  Tel. 020 8452 9823

Yoga
Yoga involves a sequence of slow, precise movements which are often stretching exercises. These exercises have a physical impact on the body – breathing becomes deeper, blood pressure is lowered and digestion improved. It is also a perfect antidote for tense muscles and joints. To find a yoga class in your area contact:

- The British Wheel of Yoga
  25 Jermyn Street
  Sleaford
  Lincolnshire NG34 7RU
  Tel. 01529 306851

Sources of Information

Recommended Books
Booth, Dr Audrey Livingston. *Stressmanship*. London: Severn House Publishers (1985).

Cooper, Cary; Cooper, Rachael D; Eater, Lynn H. *Living with Stress*. London: Penguin Books (1985).

Cooper, Cary L. *The Stress Check*. USA: Prentice-Hall, Inc. (1981).

Cranwell-Ward, Jane. *Thriving on Stress*. London: Pan Books Ltd (1987).

Greenberg, Jerrold S. *Comprehensive Stress Management*. USA: Wm C Brown Publishers (1987).

Hanson, Dr Peter. *The Joy of Stress*. London: Pan Books (1989).

Hanson, Dr Peter. *Stress for Success*. London: Pan Books (1989).

Hartley, Mary. *The Good Stress Guide*. London: Sheldon Press (1995).

Holden, Robert. *Stress Busters – Over 100 Strategies for Stress Survival*. London: Thorsons (1992).

Markham, Ursula. *Managing Stress – The Stress Survival Guide for Today*. London: Element Books Ltd (1995).

Newton, Tim (with Hardy, Jocelyn, and Fineman, Stephen). *Managing Stress, Emotion & Power at Work*. London: Sage Publications (1995).

Recommended Recordings for Stress Management
Lifestyle Management
58A Wimpole Street
London W1G 8YR
Tel. 020 7935 1965

New World Music
Freepost
Paradise Farm
Westhall
Halesworth
Suffolk IP19 8BR
Tel. 01986 781682

Useful Addresses

Alcoholism
* Alcoholics Anonymous
  P.O. Box 1
  Stonebow House
  Stonebow
  York YO1 7NJ
  Tel. 01904 644026

Bereavement
* Cruse
  Cruse House
  126 Sheen Road
  Richmond
  Surrey TW9 1UR
  Tel. 020 8940 4818

Biofeedback
* Audio House
  Progress Road
  Sands, High Wycombe
  Berkshire HP12 4JO
  Tel. 01494 511711

Complementary Therapies
* Institute for Complementary
  Medicine
  P.O. Box 194
  London SE16 1QZ
  Tel. 020 7237 5165

* Council for Complementary
  and Alternative Medicine
  179 Gloucester Place
  London NW1 6DX

Counselling Services
* The British Association of
  Counselling
  1 Regent Place
  Rugby
  Warwickshire CU21 2PJ
  Tel. 0870 443 5252

* British Association of
  Psychotherapists
  37 Mapesbury Road
  London NW2 4HJ
  Tel. 020 8452 0823

* MIND (National Association
  for Mental Health)
  15–19 Broadway

London E15 4BQ
Tel. 020 8529 2122

* Samaritans (Head Office)
  10 The Gore
  Slough
  Berkshire SL1 1QP
  Tel. 0845 790 9090

(Alternatively, see your local
telephone directory)

Diet and Nutrition
* The British Nutrition
  Foundation
  High Holborn
  52–54 High Holborn
  London WC1V 6RQ

Laughter Medicine
* West Birmingham Health
  Authority
  Healthshop
  3 Baker Street
  Lozells
  Birmingham B19 1EL

Physical Activity
* Sports Council
  16 Upper Woburn Place
  London WC1H 0QP
  Tel. 020 7273 1500

Relationships
* Relate (Head Office)
  Herbert Gray College
  Little Church Street
  Rugby
  Warwickshire CV21 3AP

(Alternatively, see your local
telephone directory)

Smoking
* ASH (Action on Smoking
  and Health)
  102 Clifton Street
  London EC2A 4HW
  Tel. 020 7739 5902

* Quitline
  Tel. 020 7487 3000
  (1–9 pm)

Stress Centres
* Centre for Stress
  Management
  156 Westcombe Hill
  London SE3 7DH
  Tel. 020 8293 4114

* Lifestyle Management
  58A Wimpole Street
  London W1G 8YR
  Tel. 020 7935 1965

* Relaxation for Living
  29 Burwood Park Road
  Walton-on-Thames
  Surrey KT12 5HL

Stress Sensor Dots
for additional supply:

Lifestyle Management
58A Wimpole Street
London W1G 8YR
Tel. 020 7935 1965

Stress Check Limited
Berean Place
Beoley
Near Redditch
Worcestershire B98 9BH
Tel. 01527 595211

Index

The Author

Alix Needham, qualified teacher, counsellor, hypnotherapist and psychotherapist, is a pioneer of the concept of Lifestyle Management and offers a comprehensive consultancy service designed to help people mould their lives creatively and effectively. She runs a successful practice in central London and heads a team of five psychologists and psychotherapists. Alix has used her experience and expertise to help numerous people from all walks of life to manage and cope with stress. She has developed and implemented teaching and training programmes on stress management in both education and the corporate sector. And she contributes regularly to TV and radio shows, national press and magazines, as well as lecturing in both the UK and abroad.

Acknowledgements

EDDISON • SADD EDITIONS

Project Editor	Zoë Hughes
Copy-editor	Peter Brooke-Ball
Proof-reader	Pat Pierce
Indexer	Dorothy Frame
Art Director	Elaine Partington
Mac Designer	Brazzle Atkins
Illustrator	Aziz Khan
Production	Lindsey Scott and Charles James